THE CONGREGATION IN MISSION

Emerging Structures for the Church in an Urban Society

GEORGE W. WEBBER

ABINGDON PRESS
Nashville ⊕ New York

3418

THE CONGREGATION IN MISSION

Copyright © 1964 by Abingdon Press

Standard Book Number: 687-09404-6
Library of Congress Catalog Card Number: 64-16152

SET UP, PRINTED, AND BOUND BY THE
PARTHENON PRESS, AT NASHVILLE,
TENNESSEE, UNITED STATES OF AMERICA

To
the
Group
Ministry,
past and present, from whose insights
and obedience the substance of this book has come

Except the Lord build the house, they labor in
vain that build it: except the Lord keep the city,
the watchman waketh but in vain.

O Lord, . . . do good in thy good pleasure . . . build
thou the walls of Jerusalem.

(Ps. 127:1, 51:18)

The substance of this book was first presented to students at Union Theological Seminary and subsequently formed the basis of lectures at the Duke Divinity School, Concordia Theological Seminary, and Fuller Seminary, as well as before various denominational conferences. I am grateful to all those who through discussion and conversation on these occasions have added greatly to my understanding and have shared in reformulating aspects of this work. A very special word of appreciation is also due to Joyce Bartlett whose remarkable labors at the typewriter have sustained me through many years.

—*George W. Webber*

CONTENTS

INTRODUCTION

An undeniable restlessness and uncertainty pervades much of contemporary Protestant church life. At precisely the time when churches have achieved quite startling institutional success, all sorts of prophetic voices, both within and without the church enterprise, are challenging the validity and meaning of much of what the churches are doing. "The need for renewal" is becoming a familiar cry everywhere, and in response a whole shelf of books on "renewal in the church" has emerged. But I am persuaded that these attempts to encourage renewal have been primarily a dialogue within the church that fails to take seriously the contour of the world in which the church is called to live and serve. There are two primary realities with which the congregation must be concerned: The gospel of its Lord and the world to which it is sent.

So far this generation has succeeded only with its inner task of theological formulation. I would suggest that hope for renewal will begin only when the congregation takes seriously the other primary reality—the world in which it finds itself, God's created world in which the church is placed for witness and service. Authentic theology emerges out of the dialogue between the gospel and the world. To serve God's purposes in our day, the churches are called to understand and share in the life of an urban culture, a difficult task when their patterns and structures had been forged in a radically different society.

In this book, then, the first concern is to examine the shape of the urban culture in which most men in our day are destined to live. We need not only some grasp of the forces that mold human life in our day, but also to ask to what degree present church life really takes them seriously. Thus we begin with an examination of what is happening to people in an urban culture that is important for the church to see, understand, and take seriously in its task of witness and service. Here the resources of sociology, anthropology, and social psychology are needed, not only to describe the reality of urban culture, but also to help the churches see their own dangerous illusions and the degree of their imprisonment in their own structures.

Brief examination is then necessary of the significant failures and blindness of present church life. Much criticism has already appeared in print without seeming to make real impact. Here I am concerned to raise questions about church life in the context of the discussion of modern urban life. As a human institution the particular expressions of the churches in a given time and place need the searching judgment that will cleanse and renew, both from the social sciences and from their own internal critics. We can accept these judgments because in faith we continue to affirm that, with all its failures, the church is also a God-given instrument that he can cleanse and renew. We speak not with cynicism or in despair, but in the hope that honest attention to our predicament may lead to a new possibility of renewal.

For the purposes of this book, modern urban life is too large a field. I propose to take a stand with the life of the inner city, but on the assumption that in the inner city one sees most clearly the problems basic to all urban life in full force. Here we are forced to look at urban life with the masks off, to look deep into the heart of American culture. The problems which one sees writ large in a slum community—juvenile delinquency, overcrowded schools, breakdown of family life, lack of meaning in work, and all the other manifestations of depersonalization—are precisely the same problems which one can read about in the sophisticated journals and the Sunday magazine section of the *New York Times*.

What is happening to youngsters in the inner city, horrifying, exaggerated, distorted as it may seem to us, in actual fact gives a picture of the kind of pressures to which the youth of our whole urban culture are subjected. This is the relevance of the inner city to the life of our whole culture. Here we see what is happening; more important, we cannot avoid seeing what is happening if we enter at all into the life of such communities.

Several further definitions are necessary. Beginning with the inner city, the basic purpose is to discover, through listening both to the gospel and to the realities of the world, what must be the shape of the church for our time. Thus the title *The Congregation in Mission* refers not to foreign missions, but to the missionary task of every congregation, rooted in the basic affirmation that the purpose of the church is always missionary, to witness in the world to the truth of what God has done in Christ. What forms must the life of a congregation assume in the city; what must its members be and do if they are to be relevant to the concrete setting in which they find themselves? We are talking here about a dialogue in which the shape of the missionary congregation must be discovered. In listening again to the world, and seeing as clearly as possible what is happening to men, the church must then ask anew about its gospel. In studying the gospel in terms of its relevance and message for our time the church is called in a fresh way to understand what is happening in the world. Out of this dialogue the congregation is called to enter into its work of mission with a genuine openness to the new forms that integrity requires —integrity to the world and to the gospel.

Missions are not an aspect of the life of the church, although this is the way they are almost universally conceived today. The church, and every local congregation, exists for mission. In God's world Christians exist as those who know that Jesus Christ is Lord and who continue his ministry of service to all mankind. They have been given wisdom and insight into the purposes of God, into the meaning of human history. They have been set free by Christ to live as new men in the world, whom nothing—including death itself—can separate from God's love. In their new humanity they are sustained by their life together in the church, nourished by its sacraments, and equipped for their work in the world. They now live to share in Christ's ministry in the world, all the time, wherever they may be, through the normal commitments of work, home, and community, as well as through the church's own instruments of service.

Such a grandiose homiletical paragraph as this, however, amounts to nothing unless the structures of the ordinary congregation are vehicles through which men may discover and experience the reality of Christian life and be equipped to live with integrity, with coherence between what they profess as Christians and the reality of their life in the world and in the church. The basic purpose of this book is to suggest structures of congregational life which may enable Christians to be open to God's grace, to appropriate a biblical faith, and to be enabled to live in the world in obedience to Jesus Christ.

The local congregation, then, is the focus of our concern. Called into being as an instrument of mission, it must exist in the world and yet be responsive to the purposes of God through the Holy

Spirit. This is a situation of dialogue and tension. The shape of the congregation must be determined both by theology and by the locus of its witness in the world. But to take this dialogue seriously must have drastic structural implications. The predicament of the church in the inner city is intolerable: The nature of the emerging theological consensus implies that much of importance in present congregational life is either irrelevant or detrimental to the missionary purpose of God's people.

As a pilgrim community, God's people must always be willing to strike their tents and move on, for mission fades whenever the church settles down for long and finds its patterns and structures growing familiar and comfortable. There is nothing sacred about present congregational structures, however hallowed by age, that leaves them free from judgment or removes them from the necessity of change. Rather, Protestants operate under a principle that requires them continually to struggle with institutionalism and are not surprised to find the sin of "morphological fundamentalism" emerging. By this term, rapidly becoming an ecumenical "ok" phrase, we mean simply the rigidity of the structures of church life. Just as the Bible is considered by fundamentalists to be fixed and unalterable, so the congregations of today, in the grip of morphological fundamentalism, assume that their present patterns of organization and activity are divinely ordained and unchangeable. In every age the church must seek from God, in the light of its situation in the world, insight into the appropriate structures for its life and mission.

In Chapters IV through VIII we propose to set forth the concrete and specific implications of our theological consensus and our cultural analysis for the structures of the congregation. In this description we are able to draw on the contemporary experience of churches that are attempting to enter into the dialogue we have been describing. But to some degree our process must be deductive and suggestive, for nothing would be more pretentious than to attempt to outline a structural program for the church as though in this way vitality and relevance might be achieved.

We can suggest, in the light of our first three chapters, certain realities which must be taken into account, areas in which the congregation must work with new vigor, points to which attention must be given in its common life. I have studied the material that is emerging from the experience of urban pastors and congregations. I have corresponded with men all over the country engaged in creative city ministries whose names were suggested by denominational executives. But the total amount of helpful material remains slender, and it has been necessary to draw somewhat heavily on the specific experience of the East Harlem Protestant Parish as it has sought to discover the missionary structures which its situation requires. At some points the dialogue between theology and the world will require suggestions of structures that at present seem to have no exact expression in parish life. We face a problem in design. But at no point do we wish to imply that structural change can be more than a tool or preparation for mission. Structures cannot guarantee the renewing power of the Holy Spirit or the ability to be sensitive to the world around. They can, however, provide an openness and new possibility of hearing and service, of responsiveness and compassion, that do not presently exist.

The five headings of the theological consensus will provide the framework for these chapters. There are direct and immediate consequences to which the congregation must give attention if there is to be integrity between theology and practice. Precisely at the point of structure and practice the congregation must be responsive to the realities of the world about it. At every point we must here be prepared to submit our proposed structures to the testing and challenge outlined in Chapter I. In a word, do these suggested structures provide a means by which the gospel will confront the reality of modern urban life, gain a genuine hearing, and provide a way through which men may discover their true humanity?

1
THE
CHALLENGE
OF THE
CITY

The congregation that wishes to fulfill its missionary responsibility must first examine the life of the city, seeking to describe and define the problems which must be of primary concern. This is not at all in order for the church somehow to learn to manipulate the city, but rather for Christians to live fully in the modern city with understanding, sensitivity, and compassion. The focus of our concern is neither to attack the city nor to defend it, but to understand it in order that Christians may witness and serve in the city with relevance and integrity.

The Nature of the City

Initially the city came into being as a place of refuge, a fortress where together men might enhance their chances for survival and worship their gods. Later it became a center for trade and commerce, thus located at a crossroads of human concourse. Finally the city became the symbol of human vitality and creativity, both the origin of and the repository for all that men prize as part of the stuff of the good life. In the familiar quotation from Aristotle: "Men come together in cities in order to live; they remain together in order to live the good life."

The modern city is not simply a larger version of urban life, however. It is in some sense a new reality that cannot be understood in historical terms alone. The vast, sprawling metropolitan areas of today represent the culmination of man's effort to shape his own destiny, to control the forces of nature, and to build a world from which God is effectively excluded. "Urbanism as a Way of Life" is the title of an article by Louis Wirth in which he discusses urbanism as representing a new phase of man's life. New words like "megalopolis" are being coined to describe the vast metropolitan complexes that have emerged.

Most important, of course, is the impact which the modern city has upon human life. An urban culture has presented us with immense human problems, bearing directly on the possibility of identity and true humanity for every man, woman, and child. We will deal here, then, with the forces at work in the city that most clearly and directly affect human beings. Let the reader ask himself to what degree these forces, here defined in terms of the inner city, do in fact shape human life in the whole metropolitan community.

Size and Density

The city of Los Angeles is spread horizontally over a huge county, while in some sections of New York 200,000 people live in little over one square mile, in vertical density found nowhere else on earth. In either case the sheer size or density of the modern city tends to create a situation beyond the control of traditional political structures. The demise of the political boss in New York City is a reflection of the vast bureaucratic structure of city government, against which the local boss becomes ineffective. One person is of no importance. At the Welfare Department people become "cases" to be serviced or numbers in a file. An old man can die in a vacant lot near Grant Houses and go unnoticed for half a day. The effect on many people is a feeling of *helplessness*, a general social disinterest, that leaves the individual feeling it is useless to participate in public life. Such people can occasionally be brought to destructive action by irresponsible leaders.

Thus size has bred indifference to human life, with the response of helplessness. Density among human beings also increases rapidly the possibility of friction, and given the initial context of poverty and segregation inherent in most city slums, the amount of conflict is inevitably large and on the increase. The human response to such pressure from other people is *isolation*. A family moves into Washington Houses in New York. Greeted by a neighbor, they respond, "We ain't going to bother nobody, and we don't want nobody to bother us." Men can indeed be lonely in a crowd.

One other aspect of the size and density of the modern city should be mentioned. This has to do with cultural homogeneity. As America has been rebuilt we have developed a variety of ghettos that almost enforce a kind of cultural homogeneity upon every group in our society. Increasingly our children are growing up in communities where those who live around them are very much the same in ideals, background, and overall culture. There is little chance for a youngster growing up in America today to rub shoulders with boys and girls of quite different backgrounds and thus gain the kind of preparation for life in a democratic community which is so badly needed.

These, then, are some of the human effects of the magnitude of the modern city. But as they are described above, it does not seem difficult to relate the same forces to suburban living. *The Lonely*

17

Crowd was not written about the inner city, but describes middle-class society. The "corporation man" knows something of loneliness and helplessness in his struggle for identity in the midst of modern economic life.

Mobility

The picture here is complex. The old mobility of immigrant communities has given way now that the inner city is peopled with minority groups who cannot so easily make the move up and out. Now the prognosis is for increasing saturation of the city by Negro and Puerto Rican groups. In 1957 *U.S. News and World Report* made a careful survey and discovered that in the previous seven years the nonwhite population of New York City had grown 41 per cent, giving the city a Negro population of about 1,063,000 and 550,000 Puerto Ricans. This rise was accompanied by a mass exodus of whites to the suburbs. Across the country the Protestant enterprise in the city is confronted with the fact that for the next generation at least, these two minority groups will be bursting across the metropolitan areas.

Patterns of mobility vary greatly in the inner city. Yet the psychology of mobility always holds good. There families *expect* to move. That is the important point. No one wants to live in a slum; so families await the day when they make a little money, or more likely when urban renewal wipes out their block. The alternative is public housing. Here transiency is relatively high, but the psychology of mobility is almost total. The woman who said, "Give me two nickels and I'll move today," was typical. In a careful study of tenants in a new project on the upper east side of Manhattan it was discovered that the new tenants, forced into public housing by site clearance, were initially unhappy people, angry at the housing authority for forcibly uprooting them, not fully understanding all the reasons for the move, lonely and insecure in a strange new environment. The people of the inner city dream of a better life and live always ready to move, but the overwhelming majority will never leave, and gradually the dreams become only an added source of misery. At the other extreme, the middle class is also on the move and just as rootless. The young college graduate who begins in Peter Cooper Village moves next to Levittown, thence to Bedford Hills, and if he makes the grade, to Greenwich or New Canaan.

The human response is *rootlessness,* unwillingness to enter into the normal fabric of community life that builds a neighborhood. It means a loss of depth in human relationships, because none are entered into with much sense of common purpose or destiny.

Rootlessness, growing out of mobility, may also have a positive side. In biblical faith Christians are often called a pilgrim people and enjoined to remember that "here we have no lasting city, but we seek the city which is to come" (Heb. 13:14). Something of the reality of these affirmations may be comprehended and internalized more easily in this day than in more stable periods of human history. In the midst of change the Christian may find resources that enable him to be at home.

Housing

On East 100th Street, between First and Second Avenues, in New York City, live nearly 4,000 people, approximately 25 per cent of them under thirteen years of age. Much has been written about this kind of slum overcrowding, with its utter lack of privacy, its exploitation, and its failure to meet minimum standards of human decency. (There are more rats— estimate 9,000,000—in New York City than people—approximately 8,000,000.)

Slum tenements, for all their problems, are now beginning to look less deadly to some urban planners as they are discovering the human liabilities of the alternative, low-income public housing. Hailed as the great solution to the need both for an excuse for slum clearance and for desirable housing for low-income families, public housing is now in something of a crisis. I believe such critics as Jane Jacobs, an editor of *Architectural Forum,* are right in calling attention to the many ways in which planning theory, concerned primarily with the "animal" needs of men—with space usage and costs and with demolishing slums—quite fully ignored the basic human needs of men, women, and children. It is interesting that political and religious meetings are not permitted in the common rooms of housing projects, thus denying to tenants the opportunity to meet for these two uniquely human purposes. The alternative is not to discontinue any form of public housing, however. The quest must be for public housing that meets the needs of human beings.

The inner city also by its housing patterns intensifies the homogeneous character of so many neighborhoods in urban areas. We group large numbers of people together on the basis of race or nationality. In the inner city we maintain, and now in public housing perpetuate, an economic ghetto as well as a racial one. Twenty-five per cent of East Harlem's slums have been rebuilt in public housing all of it for low-income families, save for one co-operative unit, struggling to find tenants. Middle-class families able to buy into a co-operative are unwilling to live in the neighborhood.

The human cost of slums, and now of projects, has often been told. Bad housing is not the sole villain in the picture of modern urban ills, as the failure of public housing to make many inroads documents. Some families struggle and do escape. Some join in fighting landlords or organizing tenants' associations. Often, however, the most descriptive word to use is *apathy*.

Several years ago a large settlement house in a blighted neighborhood was disturbed by the fact that so many of its activities were centered in its building. With the help of foundation funds it organized a program, led by a large, well-trained social-work staff, to help people who lived in crowded slum blocks do something about their problems. At the end of two years the project was abandoned, and the remainder of the funds was used to study the problem of apathy. Why had a trained group such as this been unable to elicit any response or concern from the people who lived on those grim blocks? Apathy is the overwhelming problem for many who live in underprivileged neighborhoods.

Family Life

In the inner city the family plays only a modest and often negative role as a socializing agency in mass society. There are sharp differences in the culture of inner-city groups, to be sure, but the overriding effect among the various cultural groups is the attenuation of family control. The family as the primary socializing structure of human community is rapidly losing its traditional role. By the time children reach the end of grade school other societal forces thrust themselves into the picture, giving direction and formulating their values.

In the context of poverty and slum life the instability of the family becomes a pervasive source of personal disorder. The individual on the verge of trouble seeks in vain for support from the security of such fixed relationships as child to parent or husband to wife. It is difficult at this point not to yield to the dramatic. Many exaggerated descriptions of our city youth are found in the press. In terms of sheer violence and senselessness, however, there does seem to be a qualitative difference between the city youth of today and those described in classic studies by Frederic Thrasher and William Whyte.[1] We do not really understand all that is involved in this new subculture of the inner city, but we can be sure it is related to the clearly discerned breakdown of the family.

The present almost exclusive dependence upon the family as the locus of ministry and the basic factor in the religious nurture of children is suicidal for the church. On the other hand, the experience of inner-city people with an extended family involving relationships with a good many relatives and close friends provides a preparation for life in the congregation as a family of God's people, uniting a wide range of men, women, and children. The con-

---

[1] Thrasher, *The Gang* (Chicago: University of Chicago Press, 1936); Whyte, *Street-Corner Society* (Chicago: University of Chicago Press, 1943).

21

tinuation in the inner city of some forms of looser, joint-family, or extended-family relationships is a healthy antidote to the over-reliance in American life on the nuclear, small family with its peculiar strains.

Education

James B. Conant in *Slums and Suburbs* has documented what ought to have been self-evident.[2] The schools for inner-city children are failing dismally to provide realistic education. This is not to make any assignment of the fault, for the cause will likely be found in a variety of places—family breakdown, poor teacher morale, low priority for school funds, lack of opportunity for inner-city children after schooling, and others. The present troubles of the New York City schools are characteristic of the plight of education in many urban centers. The roster of difficulties would include vast and inflexible bureaucracy; large numbers of children from non-English-speaking families; high percentage of children (70 per cent in Manhattan) from minority-group families, in this case Negro and Puerto Rican; severe retardation of pupil levels in reading and arithmetic; high dropout rate (in many New York City high schools less than half the students finish the course); high transiency rates in schools; loss of able teachers to the suburbs; lack of anything like adequate funds; and the conspicuous withdrawal of middle-class families from public education.

Conant, in language which is rather less exaggerated than we might like to think, has described the human effect of our present inner-city education as the creation of an explosive situation of frustration, incredibly costly in the loss of human potential and likely to have disastrous consequences. The children in the early grades read the same books and are indoctrinated with the same values and goals as their suburban counterparts, but the possibility of their realizing these goals is limited. Unless children recognize that education really leads somewhere—that the completion of a

[2] New York: McGraw-Hill Book Company, 1961.

22

vocational high school not only prepares one for a job, but means you will find an opportunity for which you have been trained—the mores dictate a spirit of indifference to the whole process.

The World of Work

In the fall of 1961 a seventeen-year-old Negro boy dropped out of school and began to look for a job. Not until early November, as small manufacturing plants picked up extra Christmas orders, did he find work. Hired on Monday, he went about his task with enthusiasm and hard work, only to be fired on Friday. To his dismay, he found he had been employed on a temporary basis. No employment forms had been necessary, and having fulfilled his usefulness to the employer, he was dismissed. This happened in three successive weeks. The youngster is now a drug addict.

In the inner city the pressure is as much to find work as to find meaning in work. In the new migrant family the woman often has the best success in securing employment, thus adding to the pressures on family patterns. Negro and Puerto Ricans have taken the places of previous groups in the unskilled jobs of the city, and they are far more likely to be stuck at this level, through the subtle pressures of discrimination, than were their predecessors. The lack of training in any effective skill also inevitably perpetuates the low employment possibilities of Negro and Puerto Rican youth. Further, in our chain-store society it is far harder for the small shopkeeper, so typical of earlier immigrant groups, to get started. The opportunities for individual initiative and hard work are incredibly limited.

Paul Goodman has argued in *Growing Up Absurd* that there is a close parallel in the frustrations of the inner-city youth, growing up to find no job, or one with little opportunity for advancement, and of the middle-class youth, growing up to take a job that isn't worth doing. One glimpse into the problem of work for both groups comes when you ask a child what he wants to be when he grows up. Sometimes in the inner city there is no answer at all. More often, his dream for the future is utterly unreal—a movie star, an athletic hero, a professional man (though often his heroes are less admirable characters). Goodman claims the same responses are typical of middle-class youth: "The usual answer, perhaps the normal answer, is 'I don't know,' meaning, 'I'm looking; I haven't found the right thing; it's discouraging, but not hopeless.' But the terrible answer is, 'Nothing.' The young man doesn't want to do anything." [3]

Leisure

Every society has had a leisure class, but now for the first time in history substantial leisure time has become available to the masses of men and threatens to replace work as the basis of culture. For the Greeks leisure made culture possible and was "employed" in the most important pursuits of life. For men and women in the inner city, with time suddenly given them that is not demanded either by their work or the provision for food and shelter, time becomes something to kill. Vacations for many men are frustrating and unrewarding. Some dislike time off from work. Leisure, time off from work as opposed to enforced unemployment, is now a major problem. Instead of offering needed opportunity for rest after hard work or an absorbing interest apart from daily labor, leisure has becomes a time to relax. More often, it becomes a kind of sedative, rather than an opportunity for stimulation and intellectual energy. Leisure, rather than religion, has become the opiate of the masses. In our affluent society men must endure, not work as the curse of Adam, but leisure.

For the congregation concerned about mission the fact of leisure provides a remarkable opportunity, if religious life can be rescued from its confinement to the role of helping men "kill time" and instead can assist them to use their leisure for the purposes of God's church in the world.

[3] (New York: Random House, 1960), pp. 34-35.

24

Racial Tensions

Race issues confront every part of the metropolitan community and intensify all the other human problems we have examined. The heart of the problem of race is probably most clearly defined as *rejection*. The Negro, and other minority groups, is rejected from access to decent housing in the suburbs and in large parts of the city. He is last hired and the first fired, giving rise to a tremendous loss of manpower potential for American industry. One of man's basic urges, perhaps his most sensitive characteristic, is a desire to belong. When our society isolates the Negro as a special problem it effectively rejects these people from the common life of society and augments their frustrations and torments.

The results of rejection, in spite of the obvious gains of the Negro in American life, are likely to grow more severe. Increased racial conflict is one possibility, but we are also apt to witness a fracturing of the minority groups within themselves over the racial issue. For example, the areas of justice for which middle-class Negroes are prepared to fight may be at odds with the needs of the lower class. So also in the Puerto Rican community, confronted in New York and elsewhere with racial discrimination for the first time, color has been a divisive factor, leading some to reject their heritage and others, darker skinned, to insist they are "Spanish," not Negro.

In the present crisis in race relations this country has been blessed with Negro leadership of remarkable quality. Although many of the significant leaders have in the past indicated their disillusionment with the churches as instruments of justice—Martin Luther King and the Southern Christian Leadership Conference being a notable exception—they have themselves been nurtured in the Christian faith and deeply affected by its witness to brotherhood, devotion to justice, and encouragement to nonviolent, direct action. Furthermore, the Negro churches in some communities, including their clergy, are joining in the present struggle in remarkable numbers.

The leadership of predominantly white denominations is also

taking drastic steps to join forces with the struggle for racial justice. But the challenge for the churches will have to be met not by clergy or enlightened denominational pronouncements, but by the response of local churches and their laity. When the members of a Madison Avenue church stand with their Negro brothers on a picket line it makes a far more significant witness than when ten Presbyterian clergymen demonstrate.

The time of real testing, however, will come as the dam of injustice breaks and the rapidity of change accelerates. At precisely the time when white groups are certain to feel that enough concessions have been made, the demands for even greater advances will grow more strident. Christians dare not be disillusioned by the fact of conflict, the abuse of power by minority groups, or the insistence on more and more. With understanding and genuine humility over our sins in the past, we must continue to work for a human community with justice for all men.

Depersonalization— A Legitimate Umbrella?

Running through our consideration of the problems of urbanization significant for human life there is one thread that would seem to provide a kind of summary concept. This is the reality expressed through the word dehumanization, or depersonalization. All the words we have been using— rootlessness, hopelessness, apathy, emptiness, rejection—reflect a concern for the way in which modern urban life threatens to destroy or warp the essential elements of human personality. However differently the experts may choose to define what it means to be truly human, they center in the end on the need to make cities places that fulfill human life.

In the inner city depersonalization looks like this:

A ten-year-old child looks you straight in the eye and without flinching tells a blatant lie.

A woman unmercifully beats her two-year-old child with her leather belt.

Fifteen year olds start having sex relations without then or later ever discovering the connection to love and to the mystery of selfhood.

Without necessarily using the word, the social scientists and others we have relied upon to describe urban life employ the idea of depersonalization as a correlating concept. Robert K. Merton uses the word *anomie,* by which he means a kind of normlessness, a form of aberrant behavior that "may be regarded sociologically as a symptom of dissociation between culturally prescribed aspirations (goals) and socially structured avenues for realizing these aspirations (goals)." The forces we have seen acting upon adults and especially upon youth in the inner city reveal precisely this quality. Inculcated from every side with the goals and values of our urban society, he finds no way to struggle for these ends but by short cuts, including crime and narcotics, or he capitulates to apathy. The result is anomie, a condition of life in which the true humanity of the person is denied, and the end of the process for some youth is a life of addiction, gang violence, or crime.

In his use of the term "anomie" the social scientist approaches the theologian in his use of "depersonalization." Using this concept as the basis for his own analysis of modern culture, Paul Tillich, as a Protestant theologian, demonstrates how both the secular and the theological definitions come to a point of common focus and concern.

Tillich points to a world in which not only man is depersonalized, but God is dead. In spite of tremendous lip service to God, we live in a society where most people who quickly admit to their belief in God go on at once to say that their belief has no effect upon their ethical decisions. This points to our failure either through inability, disinterest, or unwillingness to recognize the power of God upon man. It ignores the operation of God's power in history and makes no conscious effort to conform either personal or social contact to the will of God as revealed in the operation of his power.

The importance of this concept of depersonalization for our study lies in its relationship to the primary concern of the church, the renewal of man. Biblical faith insists upon the significance of every human life in the sight of God and affirms that before God's majesty all men stand judged alike as sinners redeemed by God's grace through Jesus Christ. Thus, whatever warps or limits or twists or corrupts human life and prevents it from being less than fully human is a denial of the gospel. It is the depersonalizing, dehumanizing thrust of the modern city against which we must do battle, against a culture that crosses God out of the picture by what it does to the freedom of men to respond to God as creative individuals. In the inner city the forces that dehumanize life are often direct and obvious, but in more subtle ways, the same forces seem to operate in the whole range of city life.

In such a situation the function of the church would seem obvious and its challenge unmistakable. We must now ask how, in fact, the churches are meeting the reality of an urban society. In the following chapter we shall examine briefly the way in which secular society views the life and work of the urban church. We then turn to the questions, "How are the churches relating themselves to this world of the city, and what are the crucial problems that must be faced in terms of their own structures and witness?"

2
THE
CHURCH
AND THE
CITY

To discover the image in which it is held by the world is likely to be, for any church, a discouraging and sometimes humiliating experience. A large and prestigeous Episcopal Church has stood for many years on a prominent corner in a large city. In a survey a large random sampling of all those who pass by its doors and live in its immediate area was asked the simple question, "What denomination is the church on the corner?" The great majority had no idea what denomination it belonged to, and more people thought it was a Seventh-day Adventist Church than knew it was an Episcopal Church. This was quite a shock to the congregation whose members looked upon themselves as part of the best-known church in the city.

The City
Observes the Church

The following images are not of equal weight, but indicate the various responses of the world to the church in the city, in toto, enough to give churchmen quite a jolt.

1. *Closed doors.* An executive, much traveled in cities, wrote:

In going about the country over a long period of years, I have had opportunities to observe many churches. One thing has impressed me and given me great concern. Despite all its protestations that the church stands as the servant of the people, most churches, except on Sunday, are difficult to get into. They stand seemingly aloof and inaccessible. Their doors are closed.

This indictment is true of the majority of churches which dot the inner city neighborhoods in every metropolitan area.

2. *Bastion of an alien culture.* Many of our city churches, built when Protestantism was strong in the neighborhoods, are large and imposing structures. As the neighborhoods change, and the churches continue to serve only those who come from other communities back to the church of their childhood, the building often looks as foreboding and hostile as an armory. I once visited a struggling church in a New York City tenement area where the former white congregation had almost entirely moved away. On Palm Sunday morning the entire congregation consisted of the minister and three old ladies and two children worshiping in the small chapel behind the sanctuary designed to seat eight-hundred people. Afterwards the minister and his family confessed that living as they did in the parsonage next door they felt completely isolated. The neighborhood saw them as intruders, strange and out of place.

3. *Relentless sects.* Unless one lives in a carefully guarded upper-income apartment building, his door is knocked upon frequently

by Jehovah's Witnesses insisting on gaining admittance and a hearing. For many people this comes as an annoying and pretentious attack. To those outside the church the Jehovah's Witness is completely identified with Christianity. In rejecting the teaching of the Witness, the world believes it is rejecting the gospel.

It is interesting, however, to note that in many tenement communities the Jehovah's Witnesses are welcomed with increasing eagerness. At least this visitor is deeply concerned about his faith and seems to communicate a genuine concern for the person on whom he calls. The fact that the Jehovah's Witnesses call back again without feeling discouragement or defeat explains part of their appeal.

4. *Big downtown churches.* On the other side of the coin are the large and flourishing downtown churches. What the city sees is a successful business organization operating in a modern plant and not hesitating to attract its customers by advertising its air-conditioned sanctuary. More often than not its minister is given prominent billing, not only on the sign in front of the church, but in the church ads in the Saturday morning paper. This is an institution which the world can understand, operating along lines which it finds natural and congenial.

5. *Conservative religion.* Perhaps the world sees Billy Graham at Madison Square Garden. This is in no way to make a value judgment upon Graham's religious integrity, but only to indicate that to the great mass of city dwellers who live outside the orbit of the Christian faith the goings on at the Garden are incomprehensible. It is, as one Greenwich Village group was heard to say, "The best free show in town." The world sees an archaic and rather appalling revivalism.

The city hears this conservative church on its radio. Countless small radio stations in every city in the country are supported by beer ads and religion; that is to say, by the fundamentalist preachers who support themselves in large part by freewill gifts received as the result of their radio broadcasts. This is the religion that the outsider hears in America—the insistent, demanding voice of the evangelist, using traditional religious terms that the outsider either does not understand or finds annoying or disagreeable. And when it turns on its TV set the city is more likely to encounter Oral Roberts than Ralph Sockman.

6. *A useful institution.* There are few people unwilling to see good things in the Protestant churches, but most people seem to feel that their usefulness is for someone else. The church holds family life together. It's a place to take your troubles. It's a good place to get to know people in a new community. It's an aspect of the American way of life; no community ought to be without one. "If you can't afford a psychiatrist, you might try a minister."

7. *Moral failure.* It is refreshing when a secular writer is willing to be honestly critical of the church. So few people in this day are willing to launch any kind of attack on the church. In an article in *The Nation* C. Wright Mills, then a Columbia sociologist, wrote:

Religion today is part of this sorry moral condition. . . . In the West, religion has become a subordinate part of the overdeveloped society. . . .

As a social and as a personal force, religion has become a dependent variable. It does not originate; it reacts. It does not denounce; it adapts. It does not set forth new models of conduct and sensibility; it imitates. Its rhetoric is without deep appeal; the worship it organizes is without piety. It has become less a revitalization of the spirit in permanent tension with the world than a respectable distraction from the sourness of life. . . .

The moral death of religion in North America is inherent neither in religion nor specifically in Christianity. . . .

You Christians are standing in default. The key sign of this is . . . your participation in the fact of moral insensibility.[1]

The churches, at home as well as abroad, are now also beginning to come under attack as a vehicle of white supremacy and the domination of one cultural tradition over others. The voice of

[1] "A Pagan Sermon to the Christian Clergy" (March 8, 1958), pp. 200-201.

James Baldwin, himself once a boy preacher in Harlem, has been particularly sharp in raising the question of the moral integrity of the church and in penetrating the consciousness of white Christians. In a long article in *The New Yorker* he stated powerfully the case against a church which makes proud and noble claims, but in practice denies them. He wrote:

In the realm of power, Christianity has operated with an unmitigated arrogance and cruelty. . . . Thus, in the realm of morals the role of Christianity has been, at best, ambivalent. . . . It is not too much to say that whoever wishes to become a truly moral human being (and let us not ask whether or not this is possible; I think we must *believe* that it is possible) must first divorce himself from all the prohibitions, crimes, and hypocrises of the Christian church." [2]

The white man, affirms Baldwin, is willing only to be the keeper of the Negro, not to be truly bound to him in ties of brotherhood.

8. *Divisions.* Agnes E. Meyer, in *Look Magazine,* has provided another point of insight into what the world sees when it looks at the church. She spoke vehemently of the denominational competition in referring to the "tribal habit" which besets churches, by which she means denominational rivalries and churches that are willing to help only within their own family circle. She spoke of "programs of self aggrandizement . . . resorting to the most undignified competition for converts." She spoke of the class nature of the church which has become "the expression of class distinction and racial segregation." [3] She called attention to over-churched communities. Here is really a rather desperate plea for the churches to take seriously once again their commission to witness in a broken world to the reality of God and his love for men.

9. *Innocuity.* This word is perhaps too strong, but it points to the shallow character of religious commitment in so many church

[2] "Letter from a Region in My Mind" (November 17, 1962), pp. 87-88; subsequently published in *The Fire Next Time* (New York: Dial Press, Inc., 1963).

[3] "Why Protestants Need to Wake Up," Vol. 13, No. 16 (August 2, 1949).

members. An illustration comes from a quite unexpected source, a beautiful travel folder describing America prepared by Air France:

There is also religion. Church is attended by more than 82 million people, divided into 256 Protestant sects with more than 254,000 churches. There is not much difference in European eyes between these various groups. In America, religion seems to be the supreme expression of an easy conscience.

The Urban
Church Examines Itself

We turn now to examine the city church as a problem for itself, to pick up the thread of self-criticism that is developing in church circles over the inadequacy of the witness and mission of the congregation in urban society, and to ask what difference such criticism is making on the patterns of church life. Churchmen are trying hard to diagnose their failures. It is not so clear that any effective action has resulted.

I am somewhat hesitant to offer another critique to the growing literature that attacks the failures and sins of the churches today, but it seems necessary for two reasons. On the one hand, an examination of the critical studies of the churches will give us some clue as to their relative usefulness in leading to creative change. In a preliminary way, I would suggest that the reams of criticism of the churches have created a deep-seated frustration malaise, and restlessness, but have not led to significant renewal. Will not such renewal come only through the dialogue that takes seriously both the gospel and the world, rather than through self-criticism that is not informed by a rigorous call to join in God's mission?

On the other hand, in examining again the failure of the church to meet the challenge of urban life we lay the ground work for testing the validity of the emerging structures that are being called forth by the needs of congregations that do commit themselves again to a serious missionary vocation.

34

Three areas emerge for examination: The unpreparedness of the church for life in an urban world through its dependence on rural patterns, the continual compromise, and the severe institutionalism of church life, with its concomitant pressure for success. In order, each of these problems grows more severe.

Reliance on Rural Patterns

The institutional forms of the congregation today do not reflect any clear New Testament pattern or even the style of the Reformation, but were formed in the life of a rural and small town America, a century ago. We have perpetuated ninetheenth-century patterns that served their own time well into a radically different historical context, into an age of radical change. If you return to your home church after many years' absence you are likely to find it the one familiar place in town. But it is the testimony of inner-city pastors that the traditional patterns of church life are not able to contain the ever-new wine of the gospel in an urban context.

The most frequently cited illustration of the problem of old patterns is that of the family. The churches continue to act and teach as though the middle-class family was still the basic influence on our children. *The Lonely Crowd* is only one analysis of the radical change in family patterns that have taken place. Anyone with teen-aged children knows full well that the pressures exerted effectively on our youth come far more from outside the family than from within. This fact is vastly more true for the youth growing up today in homes outside the influence of traditional Christian ideals.

Sunday-school materials and church programs, however, continue to assume that they can depend on stable patterns of family life. This is true of the curriculum materials of almost every denomination. They seem to say that unless one knows a loving father he can hardly be expected to know the fatherhood of God, and unless he has discovered the meaning of love in human relationships in a loving family he can hardly be expected to know the meaning

35

of Christ's love. Fortunately, the New Testament affirms that we know the meaning of fatherhood because we have known in Christ what it means to call God a father, and we know the meaning of human love more fully because we have known Christ's love.

Coupled with the persistence of patterns suitable in a rural society is a pervasive dislike of cities that seems to dominate the attitude of most Protestants. "New York is a wonderful place to visit, but I wouldn't want to live there or try to bring up kids," is a typical statement. Many of us in the ministry in the inner city have been almost disabled for effective work because this attitude has been so thoroughly beaten into us. To be truly human, a family needs to live in a house with a garden, in a pleasant, friendly community. We begin in the city as though we had to attack an enemy. As a small boy I attended YMCA camp. As the sun set over the Des Moines River, we sang "This is my Father's world" and learned to worship the beauty of God's created world. But it never occurred to us that God was at work in cities. This kind of bias to cities with which I began in East Harlem is almost universal within the inner city. People there have the same image of the good life as I was taught and thus want only to escape the city. Few of them will be successful, but as a group, white, middle-class Protestants have fled the city as though it had the plague. If the roughly 8,000,000 people who live in the five boroughs of New York City were assigned to the religious tradition to which they theoretically belong, about 50 per cent would be Roman Catholic, about 32 per cent Jewish, and less than 18 per cent Protestant. Of this Protestant percentage over half are Puerto Ricans and Negroes, leaving the potential white Protestants at about 9 per cent. Surveys have indicated that only about half of these are in fact related to the church, leaving New York City with less than 5 per cent of its citizens who are white Protestants. They have rejected cities and in the process left themselves ill equipped to minister to an urban world.

36

Disunity and Continual Compromise

In the city local disunity is almost universal. The struggle for survival has turned congregations inward in most cases. There are few strong church federations in this country, and at best, they tend to be the locus in which denominational groups can peer over the fence into each other's back yards or join together for the utterly disagreeable tasks which no one is willing to undertake on any other basis.

In one sense the predicament has been intensified by the most hopeful sign of interdenominational co-operation. During and particularly in the period since the Second World War most of the major denominations entered into comity agreements in regard to churching the vast new housing areas of our country. This involved a genuine commitment by the denominations involved to plan together the church building in the neighborhood, and in most cases meant that the church must try to make a genuinely ecumenical witness, seeking to reach a wide range of Protestants in the community. Unfortunately, comity which marked a step forward in church planning has also marked a sort of terminal point in denominational co-operation that has its sad effect upon the city. Denominations have become accustomed in their church extension and mission programs to comity assignments by which they take responsibility for a particular community. Unfortunately, nobody wishes a comity assignment to a difficult city neighborhood. The strategy that works for the churching of suburbia is of no use in the inner city. Here, faced by a secular world, denominational divisions become a strong obstacle to the gospel. Just as in the foreign mission field genuine unity has become imperative, so in the city it would seem that increased denominational co-operation is essential.

The selective membership of churches is a symptom of disunity. Such selectivity arises in part from the way churches are oriented to a residential community. More important, various denominations have traditionally felt responsibilities for particular groups.

Howard Hageman, in an interesting article on the theology of the urban church, quoted the church minutes of a Reformed Church in Manhattan that voted to disband in 1876 with the following words, "The moving away of the class of population in this quarter whose needs are met by such a church." This is a suggestive text for the normal pattern of church planning. We determine how many of our kind of people are in a particular community as a way of deciding whether the church extension program belongs in that community. Unfortunately in the inner city there are few people who are caught in the net of any of our denominational traditions. No one feels a particular historic responsibility for the heterogeneous multi-racial communities of Chicago and Cleveland and Detroit and New York. Hageman concluded his article with these words:

In our search for some of the theological reasons for our failure in the city, then, we can conclude that we have found at least one. It is our concept of what a congregation is. Having committed ourselves, perhaps unwittingly, to the idea that a congregation is a society of like-minded believers, we must logically place our church buildings at whatever point that society finds most convenient and desirable. The flight from every American city can therefore be said to be the result of our theory of the nature of the congregation.[4]

The deepest level of disunity lies in the class nature of congregational life. While most studies indicate that in any one denomination there is a constituency fairly representative of American society, they also uniformly document the basic homogeneity in race and culture of almost all individual congregations. There seems to be considerable recognition of this problem, but with it a sense of almost complete helplessness. In making religious affiliation a private matter, the door has been left open for people to associate in church only with those they like and with whom they have much in common. In locating churches in residential areas primarily, church

[4] "The Theology of the Urban Church," *The Church Herald* (Reformed) (November 7, 1958).

planning has made the congregation inevitably homogeneous, following the neighborhood pattern. The problem is most intense at the level of race. Gerhard Lenski, in a most revealing insight, was led to divide the American religious community, not into the usual three groupings, but into four, allowing for white Protestants and Negro Protestants. The problem involves class and cultural differences almost as emphatically, however. Gibson Winter wrote, "Studies of Protestant attendance disclose a maze of churchgoing patterns in the city, but the key to this maze is the search by middle-class people for socially homogeneous groupings, and the key to homogeneity is economic level." [5]

The impact of this "privatization" of the religious sphere on the inner-city church has been devastating. "Where leisure interests and preoccupation with family values are dominant, religious institutions flourish. Where these values are undermined by inner city life, the ministry of the churches evaporates." The life of the church simply does not intersect with the central issues in the life of the city man. In effect, the churches abandon any responsibility to the public sphere in "order to serve exclusively the emotional needs of selected groups." This divorce of the public and private spheres of life is a denial of the biblical affirmation of the lordship of Christ over the church and over the world. The result is an impoverishment and deformation of Protestantism.

At one time the parson stood at the point of intersection between the communal and private lives of his congregation, representing in his person the wholeness of God's concern for man and the fulfillment of man's life in God. Today, the pastor feels the deformation of religious life in being consigned to deal with a private sphere of symptoms rather than a public sphere of causes. [6]

[5] *The Suburban Captivity of the Churches* (Garden City, N. Y.: Doubleday & Company, 1961), p. 68.

[6] *Ibid.*, p. 165. The distinction between private and public spheres, used here by Winter, is highly important for the understanding of the dynamics of modern urban life in all its aspects. The basic study in this field is Hannah Arendt, *The Human Condition* (Chicago: University of Chicago Press, 1958).

In the inner-city churches, struggling to live amid the diversity and human life and there to witness to the possibility of reconciliation between groups and classes and the hope of ultimate unity, these patterns of homogeneity and privatization, reflected in uncritical denominationalism, are stumbling blocks of large proportion, and the pressure to appeal to culturally homogeneous segments of the community almost irresistible.

Institutional Pressures for Success

The most plaintive note in contemporary self-criticism of the churches has to do with the kind of institutional structures which have managed to evolve, and in which the churches have become encased. Again there seems to have been a kind of inevitability about the onset of this problem which leaves the churches feeling helpless. They live in a world dominated by institutions and what Kenneth Boulding calls the "Organizational Revolution." By their very nature our modern institutions are called to succeed. They cannot afford to fail, and institutional self-interest quickly becomes the sole criteria.

The churches of our time have got caught up in this world of institutions that have lost the power of effective self-criticism and achieved a considerable institutional inertia. The integrity of the church is related to its missionary purpose given by the Lord. To fulfill its function institutional patterns are necessary and right, but integrity requires that these patterns serve the purpose of the church and never become ends in themselves. At last the churches are beginning to recognize that they have become so entangled in structure that they have forgotten what their structures are for, and instead of enabling communities of witness and service to arise and function, they have sought only to become successful in an inverted, institutionalized life. Neither the failure of these patterns in the inner city nor their great success in suburbia reflects faithfulness to the gospel.

A strong word of judgment was long ago (1937) given emphatic expression by H. Richard Niebuhr in what is still an important and prophetic book, *The Kingdom of God in America*. In a chapter entitled "Institutionalization and Secularization of the Kingdom" he indicates the inevitable process by which religious fervor and awakening is channeled into some kind of institutional expression through which its values may be conserved. But they "can never conserve without betraying the movements from which they proceed." [7]

... the aggressive societies become denominations, for that peculiar institution, the American denomination, may be described as a missionary order which has turned to the defensive and lost its consciousness of the invisible catholic church. These orders now confused themselves with their cause and began to promote themselves, identifying the kingdom of Christ with the practices and doctrines prevalent in the group.[8]

Niebuhr, along with several authors of more recent historical studies, has helped the churches recognize how this present preoccupation with institutional concerns arose. In each age the church has a perspective by which it seeks to meet the world with the message of Jesus Christ, a perspective that speaks to that particular time. The church must always seek some way of relating to the world and facing the inevitable tensions that arise, even if the solution is to escape from the world through a radical sectarian witness.

In broad outlines, I would suggest that in the nineteenth century in America the main stream of our tradition affirmed that the kingdom of God was within the individual. It believed that moral men, living as those who knew within them the power of God, were the agents of God's activity in the world. This was the free, self-determined Puritan Protestant, a rugged individualist who was confident that God blessed those who worked hard and were thrifty and God-fearing. The end product was a narrow moralism, unable

[7] H. Richard Niebuhr, *The Kingdom of God in America* (Chicago: Willett, Clark & Company, 1937), p. 168.
[8] *Ibid.*, p. 177.

41

to face the emerging problems of the new world of industrialism and mass man.

Then a shift took place. In response to the growing needs of modern society the church was led to a perspective by which it sought to express the kingdom of God through institutions and a variety of voluntary organizations. The church as an institution would become the locus of the kingdom of God. In a world of mass organizations and mass culture men were led to seek salvation through large institutions and structures. Church work came to mean what we do within the gathered life of the church. Church activities and organizations multiplied, for as long as we could keep men busy within the institutional life of the church, they were secure from the tensions and compromises of life in the world. God ruled in the church, but not in the world. So the church became a ghetto, cut off from the world of politics and economics, irrelevant to the struggle of men and nations for meaning and for true humanity. The church became a human institution, judged by human standards, no longer aware of the foolishness of the gospel, where prophecy is silenced, but the new Sunday-school building is already too small. There is no tension between the church and the world because a highly secularized Christian church is cheerfully accepted by a pseudo-Christian society.

The story of religion in America for the last century and a half, then, is the story of the gradual adaptation to changing culture more than a story of a creative or prophetic force helping to shape the emerging urban society.

This "inversion of the church," in Winter's phrase, so that its mission became centered not in witness and service in the world, but in its own growth and activities, brings with it the inevitable institutional pressure for success. Insofar as this pressure is of the very nature of modern institutions, the church has not avoided this great concern to be successful in narrow, ecclesiastical terms. The marks of this trend are obvious.

1. First, people want the church to help them with their personal difficulties and needs. It becomes a service institution for its

own constituency. The inner-city pastor is enjoined to discover people's problems and see that they are met. The gospel is deeply concerned about the needs of people, but only in the light of the gospel do men know their ultimate needs.

2. The churches are preoccupied with growth and numbers. Such is the clear mark of institutional self-centeredness. They have turned from mission to the world, for which they claim Christ died, to a tremendous pressure for institutional growth and success. In the process a terrible problem has been created for the inner-city pastor, as evidenced by the long controversy over the meaning of success and failure in the church. This was touched off by a speech to a group of Presbyterian urban pastors in Princeton who were told that the church in the inner city needed to be judged, as other churches, by statistical measures and to come up to snuff. In attempting to argue against this rigid measure of the nature of the church they were charged in turn with forging a "theology of failure."

Certainly the success pattern of suburbia has presented a severe problem to the inner-city church. There is a strong tendency to assume that if only inner-city churches would try harder or find the right program pattern they, too, could be successful. Gibson Winter and others are now attacking this success orientation sharply, but the inner-city congregation still feels under pressure from the picture that Winter described:

Suburbia has introduced its concept of success into the very center of church life. Advancement, monetary and numerical extension of power —these are the criteria by which suburbia measures all things. Most church programs are now burdened with endless haphazard activity in the service of success so defined. The task of the churches as witnesses to Christ's lordship and to the power of the cross has been submerged. Clergy and laity alike are infected with the advancement ideology out of which they have grown. The test of every parish enterprise is whether it will bring monetary and numerical progress.[9]

[9] "The Church in Suburban Captivity," *The Christian Century* (September 28, 1955), p. 1113.

Recently, other important urban voices have taken up the attack on the institutional preoccupation of the church.

3. The church is run as a successful business. The church committee seeking a new pastor uses the same criteria that have been evolved by the personnel department of a good corporation. The minister has increasingly accepted the role as executive director of the enterprise of the church. He may say that he calls people into a fellowship with Jesus Christ to enter into a mission of witness in the world; yet in a recent survey 3,500 Presbyterian pastors indicated that the first thing they expect of people is an institutional loyalty—attendance, participation, financial support. No wonder the laity are assistants at best. The minister is trapped into programs where the church acts as though Christianity were a product to be sold. The vertical dimension of commitment and judgment has been eliminated.

4. Controversy is effectively outlawed. Recently a minister approached the home missions board of a large denomination with an exciting plan for expanding the ministry of his church in relationship with the business community. He was making good progress in selling the board his idea when someone asked if it had created conflict in the congregation. He indicated at once that it had created great controversy, causing a good deal of conflict and friction among the members. This simply settled the issue. He said afterwards that most of the executives present were unwilling to consider the matter further. Any new proposal that led to controversy in the church was obviously a bad thing. Let it be said that the minister himself had welcomed the controversy and felt it had greatly strengthened his congregation. For the first time in several years men and women were willing to take a matter of the church's life seriously enough to fight about it. Out of it had come a new kind of ability to face honestly the difficult issues of witness and obedience. By and large, however, anything that creates controversy in the church is taken to be unfortunate and out of place.

The inner-city pastor is in a particularly vulnerable position here. Often supported by home missions funds, he is not expected to get involved in fighting over controversial issues. To help drug addicts is acceptable, but not to start hunting down in earnest the names of slum landlords. This is a sensitive area, easy to overstate, but in reading over the materials of the denominations one is again and again impressed by the lack of concern with such areas of tension and conflict as politics, urban renewal, and housing violations.

Peter Berger comments on the same tendencies, more sharply drawn in suburbia, but real for the whole church:

It is rather a difficult feat to operate a religious establishment which exists without tension in this culture. For religion, after all, has from time immemorial been concerned with the facts of evil, suffering, and death. Yet the American religious establishment, especially its Protestant core, has succeeded in minimizing these elements to a remarkable degree." [10]

He adds in another place, the suburban church is the "community of the respectable."

Let the final word on this whole problem of institutionalism come from Charles Glock, one of the few sociologists who has given significant attention to the study of the church:

But even the casual observer of the American religious scene cannot help but note the great attention given to arranging programs, to meeting budgets, to increasing membership, and to maintaining harmony in congregations. These activities are apparently highly prized. . . . What matters, however, is the effect that emphasizing these activities has upon the fulfillment of other of the church's goals. [11]

This indictment of the church's failure and its predicament points to one overarching reality. The church in our time in the city does not confront its environment. The church and its culture are so

[10] *The Noise of Solemn Assemblies* (Garden City, N.Y.: Doubleday & Company, 1961), p. 48.
[11] Charles Y. Glock, "Afterward," Walter Kloetzli, editor, *The City Church: Death or Renewal* (Philadelphia: Fortress Press, 1961), p. 181.

enmeshed and intertwined that there is no real frontier between the two—no dialogue, no conflict, no tension. If it is the inescapable character of the gospel that it does stand in judgment over the values and loyalties of men, demanding of them an absolute loyalty that shatters the idolatries by which we seek to find meaning, then a church that is not in tension with its culture is no church at all. It is the need to confront the church again with the power of the gospel that must be our primary concern. There is a frontier between the church and the world which must be again re-established and defined, not in order to protect the church, but in order to evangelize the world.

With increasing momentum since the end of the Second World War the Protestant denominations have become aware of the problems of city life which we have been discussing. To read through their study documents is to recognize how honest they are able to be in dissecting the problems and in confessing the failure of the church to meet the urban situation.

Unfortunately, one comes to the reluctant conclusion that in America churchmen are trapped in one great besetting sin. They have come to believe that by confessing a problem loudly and longly enough, by dissecting their failures and unfaithfulness, they somehow solve the problem. The fact of complacency is seemingly intensified by the way in which men beat their breasts and at the same time continue to function along traditional lines. The very ability to be critical reassures them in their ultimate complacency. Flagellation takes the place of repentance; the problem remains untouched. Church leaders, having done justice to the critical side, inevitably proceed to tinker with the present machinery and patterns as though by adjusting the present ways of operation a bit we would be relevant to the urban situation. Structural rigidity and inertia, that is "morphological fundamentalism," is an overwhelming obstacle to renewal. In a world of tremendous change it is demanded of the church that it, too, do more than increase the efficiency of its present ecclesiastical machinery. It is my contention that in spite of the increased denominational money available for inner-city work and the great increase in genuine concern for the inner city, we have not taken seriously enough the need for a genuine reappraisal of our methods and institutional patterns.

Morphological fundamentalism is the decisive problem. So it is that we must be willing to go beyond criticism and a radical theological appraisal to take seriously the practical implications in the day-to-day pattern by which the people of God express their faith.

In actual fact, there are very few experiments that could in any sense be called radical. At the time of the Evanston assembly of the World Council of Churches, the Department of Evangelism made an extensive effort to uncover any new and significant developments in the life of the church. They were unable to come up with even a good handful of experiments in America. That, of course, was ten years ago, but even now articles about the failure of the church in the inner city almost inevitably close on a positive note, referring to places where there are signs of renewal. Time and time again there is little to point to but the East Harlem Protestant Parish, the Church of the Saviour, and one or two other spots. As a minister in the East Harlem Protestant Parish I am well aware of the fact that in almost every case the people who refer in such a positive way to this situation have never set foot in East Harlem and are only able to speak of its importance second hand. I suspect they would not dare visit the Parish for fear they would not then be able to point even to this place as a beginning of renewal!

Perhaps this chapter should end on a positive note. Unfortunately, I think we must have no confidence that there is always a pleasant conclusion to a dark picture. Later on we shall look at signs of hope in a variety of places, but in general the picture is a bleak and discouraging one. The Protestant churches, aware of the problems, critical of their own failures, must now take far more realistically the concrete steps which obedience demands.

47

3
THE EMERGING THEOLOGICAL CONSENSUS

At the same time the churches have entered into self-criticism, they have also sought to discover a new understanding of the life and mission of the congregation that would be appropriate to an urban society. Just as in an earlier day the social gospel was called forth by the confrontation of the churches with rapid industrialization and urbanization at the end of the nineteenth century, so a new theological perspective is unfolding in our own day as the churches begin to face the challenging world of urban culture and life in the middle of the twentieth century.

48

The point of urgency lies in the need for a unifying concept that would make clear the relation between the church and the world, between God and his creation. The search for a concept that would do justice to a biblical theology related to the mission of the congregation and at the same time make clear that we are not talking about some kind of mystical or "religious" reality apart from the real world of men and history has led me to the term "politics." We have already seen how the churches of our time have turned in upon themselves, in effect making the institutional life of the church the arena in which God operates. In a time of social revolution, of emerging peoples and cultures, of men and women struggling for selfhood and meaning in the face of depersonalization, we need a perspective that goes beyond moralism or an institutional understanding of the kingdom of God. This perspective will involve tension between the church and the world. It will be proximate and flexible. But we must find a posture that enables us to listen to the gospel and yet live with faith in the world.

I suggest that *politics* serve as the perspective from which to examine our theological consensus on the mission of the congregation. By politics I mean the "art of making and keeping men truly human," a definition deriving from Aristotle. In this sense politics is the crucial issue of our time; for everywhere, as we have seen, is heard the cry, "What does it mean to be truly human?" Men seek to discover what it is they need for true dignity and freedom and integrity within the life of the society in which they live.[1]

This is precisely what the Christian faith is all about. God, the Christian confesses, is at work in the world to redeem men, to restore them to their true humanity, and to maintain them in this relationship. To speak, then, of the politics of God is not only to use a metaphor but to speak of the concrete meaning of the gospel, of the reality to which Christians point when they speak of what

---

[1] For this formulation, I am much indebted to Paul Lehmann, *Ethics in a Christian Context* (New York: Harper & Row, Publishers, 1963). See especially pp. 74-101.

God has done, is doing, and will do in Jesus Christ through the church and in the world.

In this formulation we are simply affirming that God is God, that in Jesus Christ he has acted decisively in history and continues to provide the meaning of human destiny. The facts of history demonstrate that we live in an urban world. God is not putting most men in cities to destroy them, but to offer them true humanity. Once again, like the early Greeks, we dare affirm that to be a civilized man one must be a city man. Instead of attacking cities, we are called to affirm them, to love and serve them. In this way we share in God's continuing creation through the structures of human community and in the reconciling work of Christ which in the heart of metropolis calls men to their true humanity.

Using the concept of politics as a position from which to examine the mission of the congregation, we shall describe the emerging theological consensus against which the structures of the congregation need to be tested. The content of the consensus will represent what I trust is a faithful attempt to report the surprising unity that is emerging among a small group of men representing a wide variety of denominational traditions; for I am persuaded that right across denominational lines there is emerging an important agreement in the major areas of concern to the life and mission of the congregation. Here is basic material for determining the missionary structures of the congregation. This is not at all to suggest some kind of unanimity, or even a majority opinion. Rather, I believe we can find that wherever church leaders are really willing to face the failures of the church in its life and mission, as discussed earlier, they are finding theological perspectives for the work that must be done which bring men of surprisingly different theological traditions to points of common concern and emphasis.

For example, when we begin to consider our problems in terms of the mission of a local congregation, mutually helpful insights come from a variety of traditions. An Anglican, Ernest Southcott, in *The Parish Comes Alive,* inspires many Christians of widely dif-

ferent backgrounds with a new vision of the house church. The
Iona Community and writings of George MacLeod from Scotland
have led to a new emphasis on the place of worship. A Dutch layman writes a theology for the laity that is finding a response in
Protestants everywhere. The German Church through its Evangelical Academies brings new insight into the conversation between
the church and the world. Roman Catholicism through the liturgical renewal, the worker priests, and the writings on the laity of
Yves Congar, has added substantially. In these and many other
ways various Christians are beginning to learn from one another.

I am not suggesting that important elements of denominational
tradition are somehow to be obscured or ignored, but there is a
genuine openness, markedly to be seen, between our various
churches now that they are aware of their failures in the city and
the need to regroup forces for the task of ministry. Baptists are
now talking about the need to recover a deeper meaning of the
Lord's Supper; Episcopal clergymen are giving new attention to
preaching; Presbyterians are writing about liturgy and how to
enrich the worship service; and Lutherans are studying the meaning of congregational life. Congregations are discovering that the
truth they need is given to them in part from Christians who stand
in other traditions. The moment they begin to seek together patterns which will be significant in mission, they discover that they
are driven to look with fresh and penetrating eyes at their own
life and to ask the hard question: What is the gospel and what is
simply custom in the way in which we are living in our own
heritage? In a word, confronted with the thinking and concerns
of other denominations, congregations are often forced to recognize
their own idolatries and hopefully may shed them in a recovery of
what is true and relevant in their own heritage. The point of unity,
of course, is that Christ is the center for every denomination and
that in him is the source of ultimate unity.

The term "theological consensus" may seem somewhat misused,
for the source materials do not come from professional theologians.
But one can certainly argue that theology in the life of the church

is not the realm only of theologians. Hendrik Kraemer wrote in relation to his own work:

> It must, therefore, bear the mark of simplicity, free from the technicalities of professional theology. It nevertheless is theology, because every piece of coherent Christian thinking on the meaning and scope of the Christian Revelation and Faith is theology. As such, theology is not the special concern of a specialized group, but the business of *every* Christian.[2]

The basic sources from which we shall seek to demonstrate the important areas of consensus for the mission of the congregation are the speeches, reports, and writings of inner-city pastors, urban church executives, denominational mission-board secretaries, and occasional seminary professors who have sought to understand their work in reference to the inner city. The focus of our material is the mission of the church. The boundary of selection is the inner city. If there is, indeed, a consensus on significant points, then we have data with urgent implications for the concrete life of the church in our day.

God's Covenant with His People

"And take the helmet of salvation, and the sword of the Spirit, which is the word of God." (Eph. 6:17.)

The Bible confronts the church with the political perspective in a developed form. From beginning to end God is engaged in politics—ordering the destinies of men and nations. The Bible is full of political images—covenants, kingdoms, rulers, judges, and finally a Messiah who heralds the onset of a new kingdom establishing God's rule on earth. The climax of the story of redemption is political through and through. The Son who was born brings about God's rule in men's hearts; that is, makes them truly human

[2] From *Theology of the Laity* by Hendrik Kraemer, p. 104. © Hendrik Kraemer, 1958. The Westminster Press. Published 1959. Used by permission of The Westminster Press and Lutterworth Press.

according to God's purposes by reconciling them to their creator and to one another. God is at work in his Holy Spirit, not only to make, but to keep men truly human. In Christ we discover our true humanity. Thus the gospel is a "secular event." It is for the world and about the world.

With good reason the Old and New Testaments are called "covenants," for they are the story of God's dealing with his peculiar people. They are, in a sense, the constitution of the new kingdom, setting forth the basis of relationship between the ruler, Christ, and the ruled, the people of the church. Here the Christian finds the story of God at work to make and keep men truly human. For the Christian, the Bible is the locus of his search for this meaning. The church has been the key to the mystery of God's purpose for all creation. The Christian brings to his encounter with the world a unique secular wisdom. The biblical consensus thus involves a new effort to take seriously the meaning of the Old and New Testaments as a basis for understanding God's dealing with his world and the meaning of human existence. The New Testament finds its focus in the church, the New Israel, called to share in God's purpose for the world through its life of witness. The Old Testament is crucial for the life of this New Israel, for here is the concern to see what God is doing in his world. The Old Testament in a crucial way thus keeps the church from becoming apolitical.

The consensus also includes the necessity to find in the life of the New Testament guidance and insight for the missionary patterns of the congregation today. Together these reflect a rather different orientation to the Bible than is present today in much of Protestantism. One can take for granted that all Protestants, whatever the reality of the situation, will claim that they are rooted in the Bible. This usually ends up allowing every possible divergence from fundamentalism to the kind of liberalism that uses the Bible for illustrations of moral behavior. In the inner city, clergy and laity are turning to the Bible, not only for devotional help or sermon material, but for insight into missionary structures. Men are affirming that in the New Testament are patterns for the life of a congregation which must be taken as controlling or in some sense as normative. The traditional assumption of theological liberals that the Bible had little or nothing to offer at this point has been challenged. Inner-city clergy report that again and again as they seek to find new and relevant patterns for the life of the church they have stumbled upon clues in the New Testament that have led in the right direction. For example, as a number of congregations came to the conclusion that the church must function during the week in small groups and then gather on Sunday for congregational worship, they discovered in the book of Acts, the same kind of bifocal pattern of church life described: "attending the temple together and breaking bread in their homes" (2:46).

Jesus Christ Is Lord

"Let all the house of Israel therefore know assuredly that God has made him both Lord and Christ, this Jesus whom you crucified." (Acts 2:36.)

To speak of the "politics of God" is to affirm that in Jesus Christ God established a new kingdom, with Christ as ruler. This is not a new or controversial statement until one begins to ask whether this kingdom has begun and about its extent. In the consensus to which we point a clear answer is given: The lordship of Jesus Christ is a present reality. He is Lord over both the church and the world. These are difficult statements to make real—as preachers and writers are discovering—but they represent a significant theological position for the mission of the church.

God's Victory in Jesus Christ

"And what is the immeasurable greatness of his power in us who believe, according to the working of his great might which he accomplished in Christ when he raised him from the dead and made him sit at his right hand in the heavenly places, far above all rule and authority and power and dominion, and above every name that is named, not only in this age but also in that which is to come; and he has put all things under his feet and has made him the head over all things for the church." (Eph. 1:19-22.)

Seeking to break free from the assumptions of the social gospel, inner-city pastors have responded to the conception that in the life, death, and resurrection of Jesus Christ a decisive event has taken place in respect to the world. Now they are not called to bring in the kingdom of God by their own efforts, but to live in confident demonstration of God's love and victory over evil and death. This is a difficult point to make without being misunderstood. The men who provide our consensus are under no illusions about the reality of evil in the world. But now they are prepared to affirm that whether they live or whether they die, whether they can achieve clear results or not, they work with all their might in the assurance that God's victory is secure.

In the inner city, as anywhere else, such confidence in the ultimate victory of God and the assurance that has been given in Christ may lead to indifference. For the present, however, it seems to have freed Christians to work with greater diligence, for now they believe that God is at work in the revolutionary changes of the city and that they are called to take part in them. Talk about the victory of Christ may also degenerate simply into a fine sounding slogan with no efficacy in the lives of those mouthing it. The real test is the degree to which such an affirmation does indeed free the Christian to live in obedience.

Christ Is Present in the City

"For God so loved the world that he gave his only Son, that whoever believes in him should not perish but have eternal life." (John 3:16.)

In the second place, this affirmation implies a great deal about the relation of the church to the world. The traditional separation of sacred and secular is seen as false. Our present confusion about the mission of the church is, at its point of origin, a result of this

55

false division between the sacred and the secular. The church is not to be a sect group, separated out of an evil world and there, in its own purity, to be a living witness to the lordship of Christ. Christians are called to be "God's people in God's world," according to the title of a new booklet.

Such a position has decisive significance for the way in which a congregation must view its life and mission. The sectarian emphasis of much of American Protestantism is challenged by the insistence that "The Church, unlike any religion, exists to present to the world and to celebrate in the world, and on behalf of the world, God's presence and power and utterance and action in the on-going life of the world." [3] Such strident statements are reflected throughout our consensus, though often more moderately. From the publications of the Detroit Industrial Mission comes the statement,

It surely means that since God has shown us in Jesus Christ that the things of this world and the realm of man and his life and actions are God's most ultimate concerns, then we are to take the world of men and human actions as our ultimate area of concern. It means that we take our stand as men who know no higher concern than man, every man, and that we are glad to be very this-worldly, for Christ's sake.

The material of the consensus does not make clear how theological thinking in this context is able to reconcile the understanding of Christ as the risen and victorious Lord whose resurrection provides confidence of an ultimate character with the role of Christ as the suffering servant whose path the Christian is also called to follow. Such an issue is propelling inner-city pastors into the next area of consensus under this heading, the matter of eschatology.

The Period of the Beginning of the End

But our commonwealth is in heaven, and from it we await a Savior, the Lord Jesus Christ, who will change our

[3] William Stringfellow, *A Private and Public Faith* (Grand Rapids, Mich.: William B. Eerdmans Publishing Company, 1962), p. 17.

lowly body to be like his glorious body, by the power which enables him even to subject all things to himself." (Phil. 3:20-21.)

At the outset it must be clear that we are not dealing with biblical literalism or with a modern brand of premillenarian thought. As theology seeks to overcome the dichotomy between the church and the world by speaking of Christ's lordship in both realms, the tension between the present reality and the future emerges as a crucial matter.

D. T. Niles has said, "The future is already present tense. The Kingdom of the Father is already present in promise in the Kingdom of the Son." The Christian lives in the period of the beginning of the end. The end, the fulfillment, the coming of Christ in glory, is certain and, in fact, is already breaking in upon men. The church in its mission has a foretaste of life in this new kingdom. It is a token of the fullness that is still to come. This hope is the meaning of Christ's present lordship in the church and over the world.

In this chapter on emerging theological consensus we have arrived, in the concern for eschatology, at a point where the degree of consensus is somewhat limited. The controversy over the theme of the Evanston Assembly of the World Council, "Christ—The Hope of the World," revealed something of the American climate of thought. Out of the inner city, however, is emerging a clear strand of thinking that suggests in the immediate future a new emphasis upon the church as living "between the times" and an affirmation of the ultimate hope in the coming of Christ. In the inner city it is likely that this eschatological note will be a strongly biblical one, not prone to the danger of escapism or quietism, but primarily the confidence that, when man has done all, he can leave the issue in the hands of a faithful God.

The importance of this eschatological emphasis cannot be much longer denied in American church life. For the inner-city pastor and congregation it opens the doorway to a new understanding of what D. T. Niles calls the "previousness of Christ." Now, in going

57

about their business they expect to encounter the signs of Christ's presence, the fruit of the Spirit, not only in the church, but in the life of the world. The vision of the Last Judgment in the story of the sheep and the goats becomes not a threat, but a promise that one meets Christ in his neighbor. The truth is revealed that God confronts us, not in the ultimate glory of Christ, but in the ordinary encounters of daily life. He confronts us with Christ who comes in the humanity of our neighbor, with his hunger, suffering, bitterness. The church in the inner city is being judged now by its response to humanity in its midst; it encounters Christ coming to meet it now when it lives in obedience.

The Gathered
and Dispersed Life of the Church

"And day by day, attending the temple together and breaking bread in their homes, they partook of food with glad and generous hearts." (Acts 2:46.)

While the discussion of eschatology may still be somewhat preliminary and confused in the consensus to which we point, there is almost complete agreement in emphasizing the church as existing in two dimensions—in its gathered and in its dispersed life. This relates clearly to the understanding that Christ is at work in the world. Thus the church is not a building or an institution primarily, but Christians who gather here and there to worship and study but are as fully the church when they are involved in their individual relationships in the world. This relates closely to our previous consideration of the way in which Christ is seen to overcome the distinctions between sacred and secular realms.

The New Humanity

"Therefore, if any one is in Christ, he is a new creation; the old has passed away, behold, the new has come." (II Cor. 5:17.)

As the Bible is the source of knowledge about the covenant between God and his people, and as Christ is the Lord of the new
community, it follows that Christians are the subjects of Christ,
called to find their life in him. When the Christian talks about
being truly human he means to be related to Christ in obedience.
This is reflected in the frequent expression that Christ is the true
man; in him we are restored to our true humanity. On this point
the New Testament speaks with one voice. All Christians are able
to agree that the center of faith is commitment to Christ, but the
consensus that is emerging has three particular emphases in making
explicit the meaning of Christ's lordship for the individual. To
be truly human involves a conscious and life-converting relationship to Jesus Christ as personal Lord, membership in the family of
Christ's people in the context of which one discovers the full meaning of personhood and is sustained in the new loyalty to Christ,
and a new vocation on a full-time basis—that is, a life of witness
to Christ all the time and everywhere. To be truly human involves
all three aspects of life in relation to Jesus Christ. Now men accept
their true destiny as subjects of the ruler; they are God's children
by adoption.

The Gift of a New Lord

"I have been crucified with Christ; it is no
longer I who live, but Christ who lives in me; and the life I now live in
the flesh I live by faith in the Son of God, who loved me and gave himself for me." (Gal. 2:20.)

The first agreement concerns the necessity of replacing human
loyalties and idolatries, the purposeful self-determination or the
meaningless and empty existence of men, with a new center of
loyalty that is transforming. The Christian affirms that true
humanity is expressed in the life of Jesus Christ. Here is the image
of the meaning of existence, the New Adam who demonstrates the
fullness of life.

In the emerging consensus the emphasis is placed upon the freedom which is given in Christ. If a man is born in Christ, then his own human death holds no ultimate fear. He is free to obey Christ as the central purpose of his life. As Luther wrote, "Christian man is the most free lord of all, and subject to none. He is the most dutiful servant of all and subject to everyone." This paradoxical liberty makes a man truly human, for now he is free from self-deception or idolatry, and at the other extreme from apathy or cynicism or despair or fear.

Gift of a New Family

"For just as the body is one and has many members, and all the members of the body, though many, are one body, so it is with Christ. For by one Spirit we were all baptized into one body— Jews or Greeks, slaves or free—and were all made to drink of one Spirit."
(I Cor. 12:12-13.)

The new humanity of the Christian is discovered, sustained and nurtured by his life in the congregation. This is a most important point of consensus. Only as the church is a visible demonstration of the new humanity can it hope to fulfill its missionary obligation in the inner city.

By stressing the metaphor of the family, derived from Paul's Letter to the Ephesians, there is hope of escape from the present emphasis upon the church described as an organization. The focus can be upon serving, loving, caring, teaching, nurturing, rather than upon promoting, administering, indoctrinating, and succeeding. Related in faith directly to Christ, men are able to express the meaning of this faith in relation to their brothers in the faith. Free in Christ, the Christian is bound to his brothers and to the world. He is at once independent, dependent, and interdependent! All these relationships focus at the communion table where Christ is the host and where Christians stand with brothers and offer up their lives in the world.

The understanding of the nature of man and of redemption in

terms of communion not only makes sense of Paul's doctrine of the "body of Christ" and the meaning of the resurrection, but it also makes sense in terms of human awareness of the longing for solidarity and community. In a world where all men cry out against their isolation and vainly cling to mass forms of human society to protect them in their lostness, only the experience of redemption in a community of love and the understanding of themselves as men created in complete interdependence will free men to hear the good news of God's love. The new family, the fellow members of the body of Christ, are involved in a distinctive relationship and a new kind of community.

The Gift of a New Life

Therefore, since we are surrounded by so great a cloud of witnesses, let us also lay aside every weight, and sin which clings so closely, and let us run with perseverance the race that is set before us, looking to Jesus the pioneer and perfecter of our faith, who for the joy that was set before him endured the cross, despising the shame, and is seated at the right hand of the throne of God."   (Heb. 12:1-2.)

Military metaphors are often used these days to describe the life of the Christian. To accept Christ as Lord is like entering an army. Christ becomes the general. The church is the full company of troops, and the purpose of this new military life is to fight the battles of the commander. Thus, in accepting Christ as Lord the Christian really takes on a new vocation, that of a soldier in time of war who must devote all his time and energy to the pursuits of battle. This leads, of course, to a new consideration of the doctrine of vocation: "What can it mean to say that for the Christian both his gathered life in the church and his life in dispersion must be fully at the disposal of his Lord."

The Ordering of God's People

"But you are a chosen race, a royal priesthood, a holy nation, God's own people, that you may declare the wonderful deeds of him who called you out of darkness into his marvelous light." (I Pet. 2:9.)

The laity are the people of God, called to be his "politicians" in the world. The clergy exist within the church to serve God's purpose for ordering and directing his people for their ministry. The renewed concern for the role of the laity has been a concern of very great prominence in the theological consensus. One indication of this widespread trend is seen in the publication some years ago of *Lay People in the Church* by Yves Congar, a Catholic priest. From Roman Catholicism through the spectrum of Protestant denominations has run this emphasis on recovering the witness of the laity. Much of this attention to the laity can end by doing nothing more than galvanizing them into even more frenzied action, as Hendrik Kraemer has observed. In terms of the mission of the congregation, however, there are three areas of importance to be noted fairly briefly. I do not believe that any very great documentation is necessary, but I do wish to underline the points of significance.

The Priesthood of All Believers

I appeal to you therefore, brethren, by the mercies of God, to present your bodies as a living sacrifice, holy and acceptable to God, which is your spiritual worship. Do not be conformed to this world but be transformed by the renewal of your mind, that you may prove what is the will of God, what is good and acceptable and perfect." (Rom. 12:1-2.)

Often Protestants seem to speak of the priesthood of all believers only in anti-Catholic discussion. Now more frequently this biblical doctrine, recaptured by the Reformation and then lost in practice in the life of most churches, is seen to speak of the ministry of the whole church. Christ's ministry is continued by his body. An Anglican bishop wrote: "All that is said of the ministry in the New Testament is said not of individuals, nor of some apostolic college or 'essential ministry,' but of the whole body, whatever the differentiation of function within it."

62

In the second place, the priesthood of all believers is concerned to speak about the gifts of the Spirit given to the congregation. The basic texts come from I Cor. 12 and from Eph. 4.

In the third place, to speak about the priesthood of all believers has come to involve a recognition, rather strange and new to many Protestants, that a priestly function is involved. This doctrine is not primarily oriented to a doctrine of the laity but is concerned with the priestly ministry of God's people. The basic text is, thus, "bear one another's burdens" which includes mutual ministry and intercession. All God's people are called to offer themselves as living sacrifices to Christ and to pray for their brothers. They must share in the struggles of their brethren, coming as one who brings Christ's love.

Doctrine of the Laity

"And his gifts were that some should be apostles, some prophets, some evangelists, some pastors and teachers, for the equipment of the saints, for the work of ministry, for building up the body of Christ." (Eph. 4:11-12.)

Hendrik Kraemer's *A Theology of the Laity* is already something of a classic. Unlike Arnold Come's *Agents of Reconciliation,* it does not raise the question of ordination in any sharp terms, and thus avoids the most divisive issue in this whole area. What Kraemer affirms, and most inner-city men now accept, is the statement: "The ministry of the church is given to the *laos.*" It is the laity, living and involved in the world, on whom Christ's basic ministry of witness and service devolves. They are the "frozen" assets of the church, already present in the world, who must be thawed out and set about their rightful business right where they already are. As we shall see again later, the concern of many is to cut across the usual secular-sacred split. Kraemer wrote:

The paradoxical situation in which the "world of the Church" finds itself is that on the one hand it has to purge itself from much insidious secularization or worldliness, and on the other hand has to become really worldly, i.e. open to the world and its real concerns and perplexities. In other words, it has to become in a new way un-worldly and worldly in one.[4]

Along with the emphasis on the laity as the church alive in the world is the stress on their role as full participants in the gathered life of the church. Called to obedience in the world, in the church's life together they are called to acts of gratitude. Wherever laymen are taking their life seriously, the worship of the church comes alive, for now they are part of it, not spectators.

Again the doctrine of the laity emphasizes that Christians are called into full-time service. Several writers have pointed out that the word *sacramentum* refers to the oath of allegiance taken by the Roman soldiers enlisting in Caesar's legions, and the word *paganus* referred to civilian life. In this metaphor, by his sacrament of baptism, the Christian is ordained to a new way of life, to a ministry in Christ's name. He goes from a civilian to a military life. Now he is a man under orders. For the Christian it is always a wartime situation; he must be on duty at all times and in all places.

Doctrine of the Ministry

"For if I preach the gospel, that gives me no ground for boasting. For necessity is laid upon me. Woe to me if I do not preach the gospel!" (I Cor. 9:16.)

If, as a Lutheran document affirms, renewal depends upon "a bold venture in the direction of re-establishing the laity as active participants in the ministry of the Church as over against the widely prevailing ideas that they are merely objects of a clergy-centered ministry," this kind of conviction means also some radical changes for the clergy. As Arnold Come insists, the laity will

[4] *Op cit.*, p. 166.

not be treated with necessary seriousness or with any integrity at all while the present image of the clergy's role is maintained. If we insist that there is only a functional difference of services between the clergy and the laity, as most denominations short of the Episcopal are prepared to do, then we must align the structures of the church to insure that all mature Christians may exercise their full ministries.

In large part the ministry of the laity is in the world, while that of the clergy is in the gathered congregation. Both, however, are part of the one mission of the church in and for the world. This is a distinction acceptable to clergy even in the Episcopal tradition. "The clergy's part is to preach the Word of God but to accept also their dependence upon the laity and their involvement *in* the world for effective communication of the gospel *to* the world." [5] Thus we may agree that ministry involves both clergy and laity, however we may differ in the meaning of ordination. There is considerable agreement with what H. Richard Niebuhr called several years ago the emerging concept of the minister as the one set apart for preaching, the administration of the sacraments, and the equipping of the saints for the work of ministry. From this perspective the work of ordination is within the gathered life of the church, with certain clearly defined functions that by no means begin to cover all the needs of ministry in the church.

A matter of particular debate at the moment concerns the role of the clergyman as pastor. Insofar as this makes him into the chief counselor of the congregation, most inner-city ministers find this an impossible role and are willing to argue that it also severely undercuts the reality of the priesthood of all believers; that is, of a ministering congregation. Rather, they would suggest that the clergyman is called to realize and direct the gifts of spiritual care that are given to the members by the Holy Spirit, rather than to center this function in himself. More important, we need a new definition of the pastoral role of the clergyman. In effect, as pastor

[5] Reuel Howe in *Newsletter*, Institute for Advanced Pastoral Studies (May, 1962), p. 4.

the minister is called to give time to prepare and equip the members for their ministries in the church and in the world. Only as we make a sharp distinction between this type of pastoral work and the quite different, though legitimate, role of the personal counselor, can we disentangle the clergy from the present demands upon them and give them freedom to fulfill their proper and urgent role in giving direction to the mission of the congregation.

The Church Exists for Mission

". . . and designated Son of God in power according to the spirit of holiness by his resurrection from the dead, Jesus Christ our Lord, through whom we have received grace and apostleship to bring about obedience to the faith for the sake of his name among all the nations." (Rom. 1:4-5.)

The most obvious theological consensus today concerns the function of the church. The commonly used phrase is "the church is mission." In the light of the problems of institutionalism which have been so much on the conscience of the churches it is no wonder that today they respond to an emphasis which seeks to turn congregations away from an introverted and self-centered concern to face a task that serves the world. In heeding the call of Christ, as we have seen, the Christian accepts a new vocation. The church and all its members exist, are called into being, in order to enter into the ministry of Christ in and for the world. The church is to be recognized by its missionary character—by the extent to which it reflects the fact that it is God's church and has accepted the mission he has assigned it.

One can see the gathering momentum on this consensus in the literature of the last fifteen years. In this country Truman Douglass, in many of his speeches, began to quote the fine phrase of Emil Brunner, "A Church exists by mission as a fire exists by burning." In ecumenical circles this emphasis, with its biblical basis and theological meaning, developed rapidly and gained a general acceptance beginning with the important missionary conference at Willingen and gaining momentum at Evanston where the discussion of both evangelism and laity centered around the theme "The Evangelizing Church." Typical of the statements was: "Everything the Church does is of evangelizing significance. Through all the aspects of its life the Church participates in Christ's mission to the world, both partaking of the gospel and seeking to communicate it." [6]

As an attempt to find a posture that would recall the life of the churches to its true purpose, this emphasis on mission was a helpful note to sound. But in its simple form, "The church is mission," it leaves many questions as to its meaning and application. The very need for self-correction in the church can readily lead to a certain sloganizing that itself is a source of misunderstanding. "The church is mission" must thus be seen in the consensus as an important emphasis, but not as an absolute and all-inclusive formula.

In seeking to give some order to this discussion of mission, I suggest that the political metaphor by which we have organized this chapter can be of further help. In large part the present validity of the affirmation "the church is mission" depends upon the degree to which it helps lift us out of organizational preoccupation and, at the same time, provides a basis for overcoming the present dichotomy between the church and the world. The mission of the church is to make and keep men truly human. For this purpose the church exists. In this sense the church is the agent of God's politics. In its gathering and in its dispersion, it is an instrument of God. In both dimensions God's task claims it. *In short, evangelism, in its varied dimensions, is politics.*

Discerning the Activity of God

"For he has made known to us in all wisdom and insight the mystery of his will, according to his purpose which he set forth in Christ as a plan for the fullness of time, to unite all things in him, things in heaven and things on earth." (Eph. 1:9-10.)

[6] *The Evanston Report* (New York: Harper & Brothers, 1955), p. 100.

In Christ, God is at work in the world seeking to make and keep men truly human. The first task of Christians is to discover where he is at work, in the faith that God has revealed to the church the meaning of life and history. Thus, in the gathered life of the church we have already noted the strong emphasis upon biblical study and preaching, for this is the locus of the search for meaning. Here is God's Word, in a way of speaking, the battle orders for his people as they seek to enter into his work.

It is a far harder matter for the church to know what it means to look for God's activity in the world, but the affirmation that Christ has been made head over all things and given all authority is beginning to find further theological explanation. Often quoted is the statement of George MacLeod: "You must read your daily paper to see what God is doing in his world, and how the forces of evil war against him." Charles West's book entitled *Outside the Camp* makes the point that the church is always called to strike tents and join God outside the gate (Heb. 13:12-14). In *Presbyterian Life*, Markus Barth is quoted as saying:

> I would say that since Christ is outside the gate, sent from the Father, we will be with him insofar as we, too, are sent. And we will find him, apparently, not in Jerusalem, but outside the gates, precisely among unbelievers. We ought to announce something along this line as a goal for Sunday school.[7]

In the consensus, then, we discover an emphasis upon the fact of God's activity in the world and a conviction that the Christian is called to discern the Word of God in the world. This power of discernment is the unique, essential mark of the Christian. "The cohesion and commonalty of the vocation of Christians originates in their power to discern the truth of the Word of God in any event whatever, and precisely because the Word of God is present in all events, that power may be exercised in any event." [8] In this sense the church does not introduce God to the world, but is solely con-

[7] *Presbyterian Life* (October 1, 1961), p. 24.
[8] Stringfellow, *op. cit.* p. 42.

68

cerned to introduce the world to God; that is, exposing through "the discernment of . . . , the reliance on . . . , and the celebration of . . . , the presence of the Word of God in the common life of the world." [9] Such statements as these have a vague and perhaps hollow ring. In many places and many ways, however, inner-city Christians are seeking to give expression in one way or another to their dim glimpse that God is indeed ahead of them and they must find the signs of his presence. Thus involvement in the life of society self-consciously as a Christian is not so much a matter of obedience as a condition of being in communion with God at all.

Entering into God's
Activity as Obedient Instruments

"The Spirit of the Lord is upon me,
because he has anointed me to preach good news to the poor.
He has sent me to proclaim release to the captives
and recovering of sight to the blind,
to set at liberty those who are oppressed."   (Luke 4:18.)

To see what God is doing is a call to participate in the drama of salvation, the task of making and keeping men truly human. Now the focus for the church is not primarily the moral life nor on the building of an institution, but living as "agents of reconciliation." Accordingly, witness is nothing else but "participation in the work of God . . . which He is doing all the time and everywhere." [10]

In the gathered church, as we have already emphasized, this participation is a call to be the church, to express the reality of our true humanity, living together as a family and demonstrating the unity in Christ which transcends all human differences of class, culture, and education. In the church men are called to live as those who have already entered the kingdom of God. God is ruler indeed as Christians learn to speak the truth in love, to bear one another's burdens, and to worship their Lord.

[9] *Ibid.*, p. 56.
[10] Hans Jochen Margull, *Hope in Action* (Philadelphia: Muhlenberg Press, 1962), p. 59.

In the world, where God has placed the congregation in dispersion as his servants, the members are called to enter into his work of healing and reconciliation between men and nations, to work for justice and opportunity for all, and to live as those who are in the world and yet ruled by the authority and power of a heavenly Lord.

The strong note, as indicated above, is that Christ is present in the world. We do not say to the world, "Come and be like us"; we say, "Christ is willing to be with you where you are." This presence is made real in the *diakonia* of Christians. The point of meeting with the world is not only in Christ's presence, but also in our common humanity.

Christ is the light that lightens every *man*. My point is that the Christian . . . is not going out to enrol men under the banner of a tribal deity. We are not inviting strangers to come into our house. We are asking all men to come to their own home where they have as much right as we have. . . . [Christ] is not the head of religion, but the head and King of the human race.[11]

In this framework, the church is seen as continuing the ministry of Jesus as described in the New Testament—healing, teaching, discovering a beloved community, sharing fully in the life of the world. More important for our purposes, such a theology also develops an awareness that the Incarnation leads to a cross. It is a path of suffering, suggesting a note that has until recently been rejected by the American churches as a necessary part of Christian obedience.

Pointing to
the Presence and Power of God

". . . and to make all men see what is the plan of the mystery hidden for ages in God who created all things; that through the church the manifold wisdom of God might now be made known to the principalities and powers in the heavenly places. This was according to the eternal purpose which he has realized in Christ Jesus our Lord, in

[11] Lesslie Newbigin, *A Faith for This One World* (New York: Harper & Row, Publishers, 1961), pp. 65-66.

whom we have boldness and confidence of access through our faith in
him." (Eph. 3:9-12.)

When Christians gather to worship and study, either in a
church building or in their homes, they become a visible reality
which even in some broken and partial degree can reflect the glory
of Christ. In a gathering of Christians who are learning to live
by grace there is a quality, a style of life, that may make a witness
to those who come among them. A missionary congregation dis-
plays the first fruits of the kingdom.

When, in dispersion, the congregation enters into the life of the
world they also pray that there they may be a witness that points
to Christ the Lord. This emphasis rightly comes in the last place,
for in a world of constant talk, where men too easily chatter aim-
lessly or assume the role of spectator, the church does not dare add
its own chatter or talk irrelevantly in words the world no longer
understands nor cares to hear.

The forms of pointing which one hears mentioned in our consensus involve first of all "gossiping the gospel." This is the natural
response to Christ of men who have been made captive to him.
Something of such overwhelming importance has happened to
them that naturally, without sounding forced or intruding into
the lives of others, or even seeking any response, they "gossip"
about that which is of ultimate importance to them. This theme
was the subject of Lenten Bible study in inner-city parishes in
Lent, 1962.

A second aspect of pointing is to stress the need for Christians
to enter into conversation first at the level of their common humanity with others. In learning to be human with other men, to
converse at the level of genuine meeting, the way is prepared for
communicating the meaning of faith. This is the point of Kraemer's
widely read book on communicating the Christian faith. Said another way, it means keep quiet until the world asks the questions.
This need not contradict the idea of "gossiping the gospel" but
serves to remind the Christian that he must be sensitive to the

other person, not an intruder. An illustration comes from an inner city pastor in Holland:

In 1948 the first gangs came to our buildings. . . . It has been very useful to wait. We refrain from trying to Christianize those visitors after our own manner. We wait for the time when they come and ask us to render an account of the faith that is in us. We believe that the church must wait until this question is asked.

In the third place, the congregation is concerned in all it does to point to Christ and not to itself. "Let your light so shine before men, that they may see your good works and give glory to your Father who is in heaven." (Matt. 5:16.)

Fourth, the congregation awaits the end. Its mission of witness is until the Lord comes. This eschatological note has clearly intruded itself, as we suggested earlier, into the inner city enterprise in this country. It is the hope of Christ that makes possible strenuous efforts to share in the heartbreaking work of Christ, and yet does not depend upon results. "There is, however, no anxiety about the only Victory that is important. Christ has already overcome the world. We follow in His train, stumbling, weak, blind, but with devotion." [12]

Finally, to point to Christ is to trust that he alone converts and calls men. He is the evangelist. Men only share in his work. At Evanston it was said, "We must remember that evangelism is God's work in which we are His agents. It is not our work, and therefore we must wait upon Him in prayer and in meditation upon His holy Word, that we may learn what He would have us do." [13]

In this chapter we have tried to point to areas of agreement on matters that are essential to the life and mission of the church. These are all areas that have become urgent matters as the church has faced its mission in an urban culture. In these areas there is great

[12] Robert W. Spike, "Historic Judson Church in Greenwich Village," *The City Church*, September-October, 1954, p. 5.
[13] *The Evanston Report, op. cit.*, p. 101.

agreement that cuts across denominational traditions, wherever men face the realities of the modern city in all the great communions of Protestantism. The problem is not at this point but precisely the desperate need to translate our common theological presuppositions into concrete expression in the life of the church. We have a tremendous ability to formulate powerful theological concepts, but in actual practice our lives as Christians in the church and in the world continue in the same old ways. It is the purpose of this book and the focus of the rest of our study to try to take seriously these theological affirmations and to seek to discover what they suggest as to the way we must live in our life as Christians amid the realities of the world.

Both our critical examination of the present patterns of the church's life and our theological consensus are important only as we go one step further and become involved in a continuing search for new forms of the life and mission of the congregation today. In the following chapters we shall in turn examine the concrete implications of each of the five elements of the emerging theological consensus for the structures of a congregation that would be used by God for his work in the world.

And I saw the holy city, new Jerusalem, coming down out of heaven from God, prepared as a bride adorned for her husband; and I heard a great voice from the throne saying, "Behold, the dwelling of God is with men. He will dwell with them, and they shall be his people, and God himself will be with them; he will wipe away every tear from their eyes, and death shall be no more, neither shall there be mourning nor crying nor pain any more, for the former things have passed away." (Rev. 21:2-4.)

4
THE
LIVING
COVENANT

We turn now to five chapters in which we shall examine the response of the congregation in its self-understanding and organizational patterns to the dialogue between the gospel and the world. In this chapter, we begin with the first element in the consensus—God's covenant with his people: the Bible as controlling in the life of the congregation—and ask what are the implications of this affirmation for the congregation that is trying to live with integrity.

A report from an inner-city parish reads:

After eight years of work in this situation, we have come to the conclusion that we must limit much of the present program and activities of our ministry and give major attention to Bible study. We simply do not know how to proceed or to what we must give priority. We are convinced that we are literally being driven back to first things.

With this note of urgency, almost desperation, Protestants are turning anew to the study of the Bible. As we have seen, in the theological consensus there is solid agreement that the Bible must have a normative place in the Christian life.

Protestants are people of a book. The Reformation was a strenuous calling of the church back to the faith of the New Testament. This is in no sense a biblical literalism, but the inescapable fact that the faith of the church is rooted in the revelation of God in Jesus Christ and that this revelation is made known primarily in scripture. The excitement of the Reformation came in large part through the translation of the scriptures. Now for the first time men could read and hear the word in their own tongue. In Geneva, Calvin presupposed a Bible-reading congregation that, through its knowledge of scriptures, was able to do its part by defending the word against the preacher. Men who took their faith seriously studied the true and lively word. The contours of faith were familiar to them. This was true for many Protestant households several generations ago. The Bible was a book read and studied. Its stories were familiar landscape to children and adults alike.

Today every survey points to the abysmal illiteracy of most Christians, including many ministers educated at our inter-denominational seminaries, where they study about the Bible but read little of it. The real problem is the fact that clergy and congregations accept biblical illiteracy as a given situation, as sort of a fate which must be expected and with which they are hardly concerned to struggle since there is so little hope of changing it. This would seem to be intolerable.

Bible study with a difference thus appears to be the first "missionary structure" of the congregation, basic to the other aspects of its life. The word "study" is usually taken literally, for the only kind of Bible study that seems to make much difference in a church involves discipline of mind and hard work. Clergy are well aware that sheer ignorance of the Bible may be just as harmful as rigid fundamentalism or even the kind of pseudo-literacy that enables men and women to recite the facts of the biblical story without in any way finding in God's covenant the basic constitution for their lives.

In missionary congregations the study of the Bible as a living covenant involves at least three objectives. First, the Bible defines for the Christian the political order in which he lives. Here is set forth the nature of the relationships between God and his people, the meaning of his rule and of the lordship of Christ. The Bible is not concerned primarily with subjective "self-understanding," but with the reality of God's dealings in the light of which man only truly understands himself and his world. In the second place, the Christian seeks to appropriate the events in the history of the Old and New Israel as his own personal history. Just as the liturgy of a Jewish household revolves around the re-enactment of the salvation events of Israel's history, so for the Christian the life of the Old and New Israel must become his personal life history, beginning with Abraham as his great-grandfather many centuries removed. In this way the covenants of God with men may become the basis of his life relationships also. In a congregation that studies the Bible in this way, as personal history, mutual relationships may begin to come alive in the terms of a family. Third, the study of the Bible is being directly related to the present and the future, what the man of faith is to do and for what he is to hope, in the congregation and in the world. Only men and women "drenched" in scripture can hope to see the world through eyes of faith, to discern the Word of God in secular events. The "sword of the word" is the only offensive weapon listed in the catalog of arms in Eph. 6. For Jesus the word of scripture was again and again his defense (as in the temptation stories). So for the Christian his defense against the enemy lies in his use of the "sword of the word," not as a fundamentalist quoting proof texts, but as a living confidence in God who is always faithful.

In this chapter we shall begin with a description of a concrete pattern for Bible study designed as a long term plan to enable adults to live under God's covenant with understanding. This is followed by a section on the relation of Bible study to preaching. The chapter concludes with a word about the implications of these patterns for the missionary structures of the congregation in the light of the realities of the city.

Adult Bible Study

The pattern described here has emerged in a group of inner-city parishes in New York, Chicago, Cleveland, and elsewhere over the past ten years.[1] In each case, not only was any biblical perspective found to be foreign to the congregation, but also the people were quite ignorant of the basic facts of the life of Jesus and the early church as well as of the history of the Old Testament. Church officers were willing to admit the truth of this situation and to begin an objective effort to involve their congregations in Bible study in order that they might know their way around the biblical records. The clergy, of course, devoutly hoped that other vital by-products might emerge in the course of study—deepened faith, perhaps a second conversion, personal appropriation of *heilsgeschte,* and a new depth in the experience of unity and fellowship in the life of the community of faith. But the start was made at the point of a forthright attack on ignorance and illiteracy. This was to be a long-term approach, for only through such a commitment did they feel there was any hope of keeping people at the task during the difficult early months while Bible study had not yet become a normal part of congregational life, a "habit" of the Christian style.

[1] "The Bible in the Parish," *News Letter,* East Harlem Protestant Parish (Spring, 1960). For a listing of various reports and articles published by this parish, write to East Harlem Protestant Parish, 2050 Second Avenue, New York 29, New York.

Methodology proved to be important, particularly if Bible study were to be made a central part of the commitment of the congregation.[2] The first key is a new conception of the role of the clergy. Given the training of the ministry and the traditional spectator role of laity, Bible study often quickly turns into a situation in which the minister teaches the group about the Bible. Quite different results have been achieved when, instead, the whole group, including the clergy present, come together under the Bible and together seek its meaning for their lives. The clue is for the minister to keep silent, particularly at the beginning, as a way of leading others to reflect and speak. His role is best seen as a resource on technical questions of definition and word meaning. When Christians seek together to read God's word and appropriate its meaning for their lives no one person has a unique role, particularly when it comes to personal appropriation and relevance. In the inner city parishes the clergy or other staff present in Bible study play a significant role in directing discussion and clarifying issues, but they kill Bible study when they intrude themselves between the Bible and the group and turn the meeting into a classroom.

In the second place, methodology now being developed suggests that it helps to follow a consistent study pattern for a substantial period, either going straight through one book of the Bible or working through a coherent theme. This plan is central for the inner-city lectionary called *Daily Bible Readings*.[3] Published quarterly following the church year, it devotes a quarter to a book of the New Testament, one to part of the history of God's call to Israel, and the others to the themes of the New Testament urgent for today, such as Christian family life. In this way, over

<hr />

[2] On methods see "Guiding Principles for the Interpretation of the Bible, as accepted by the Ecumenical Study Conference at Wadham College, Oxford, 1949," reported in Alan Richardson and Wolfgang Schweitzer (eds.), *Biblical Authority for Today* (Philadelphia: The Westminster Press, 1951), pp. 240-44.

[3] In terms of the Bible study lectionary, a number of inner-city parishes have together worked out a lectionary, published quarterly, covering a four-year period. It is designed for weekly study along the lines outlined here. *Daily Bible Readings* published co-operatively for the Inner City Parishes by the East Harlem Protestant Parish, New York.

the course of some years the congregations are led to a firsthand knowledge of the books of the New Testament and the basic history of the people of Israel and to much of the biblical insight into the problems of daily life.

The third key to Bible study emerges in the procedure of the sessions themselves. The inner-city parishes have found that study must be on a weekly basis if it is to be taken seriously and to make much progress. The general procedure for an individual session is to begin with a prayer and then read aloud the passage for the week. There may be people present who cannot read, and, too, most inner-city people are more accustomed to hearing than to seeing words. After several minutes of silence for reflection the whole group is asked to speak briefly on such questions as these:

1. What don't you understand about the passage, or what in it is confusing?

2. What is the most important point in the passage?

3. Do you agree with the point of the passage?

4. How does this passage speak to our problems today? The questions may be varied, but the point is to begin by seeking the involvement of all present in the discussion, not with a lecture on the historical context and the theological significance of the passage, followed by suggested questions for discussion, all by the minister. The concern is directed to the need for men and women to learn to study the Bible, to hear its message, and to live in its perspective as their own mode of life. Someone, just the same— and it may be a layman—needs to come prepared to deal with critical problems that may arise in the text. This means diligent preliminary study with commentaries. In a situation where laity are competent in teaching, clergy have found it practical to give their time to one weekly Bible study meeting for leaders of the various groups in the parish. Such a Bible study training session would equip the lay leaders responsibly.

Such preparation is for assistance when necessary, however, and has no place for its own sake in the discussion. This point is easily misunderstood. Bible study does not consist of pooling ignorance, and often depends upon the immediate availability to the group of solid, critical research. Such resources are called into use only as needed, however. Basically this pattern of Bible study assumes that when men and women, with some openness, enter into this enterprise the biblical material does come alive and through the power of the Holy Spirit God does make himself known in the lively power of his word.

It is often very difficult to persuade people, particularly long-time church members, to respond honestly to the Bible. They usually feel they must swallow the passage whole, no matter how strange or even ridiculous it may seem. The best Bible study groups are likely to be those to which come several people who are quite unconvinced of the truth of the faith and the relevance of scripture. Their honest reactions can frequently open up others to admit their hidden questions and objections. Only as men respond to God's Word honestly, without any superficial piety, is there much hope that they will probe to the real meaning of a passage.

Several other details of methodology have emerged. The best size for such a group seems to be ten to fifteen. The study session usually lasts about an hour and a half and is followed by coffee and cookies. Often the informal discussion continues for another hour. Most of the groups meet in the evening, beginning at about eight-thirty. Experience also indicates the importance of meeting, not in church buildings, but wherever possible in homes. This makes clear again that the congregation must live and enter into its witness in the world and that the church's business is not only what is done within the church building.

This pattern of Bible study now has a good deal of experience behind it. The inner-city parishes as well as some thirty other congregations now use *Daily Bible Readings*. The testimony from these situations indicates that there are significant by-products for a missionary congregation in this kind of corporate study of the scriptures. In the first place, Bible study provides a context in which *koinonia* may be discovered. In the context of regular Bible study men and women find it hard to maintain their disguises. Often in the study of a particular passage those present cannot hide from those who know them well. For example, when some groups were studying the problems of the church in Corinth in the early chapters of First Corinthians, many present were deeply troubled by the sudden recognition that Paul seemed to be directing his words to them. A process of divine restlessness was set loose which helped drive one congregation from complacency and forced it to ask more searchingly about the business of the church in this day. One minister reported that nearly six months later in a session meeting one elder, in the course of a tense discussion, said, "But that's exactly what the church in Corinth was up against." This kind of personal involvement and appropriation makes possible relationships of understanding and honesty. No relationship of love can develop unless there are structures in which it can grow. This is not to overlook the hostilities, bitterness, tension, and all the rest which will emerge as men and women are stripped or strip themselves of their masks and defenses. For all the dangers of the dynamics thus released, however, the inner-city parishes do not seem to have bogged down in personality clashes or individual problem-people that disrupt the groups. This may be in part due to the objective study character of the meetings. These people do not come together for therapy. But the members would affirm that when a group of Christians meet in the expectation that the Holy Spirit will be present, then love and unity and new truth may break forth that will enable them to venture upon the task to which they have set themselves in spite of all the hazards.

Another often reported effect of Bible study is what John Wesley called a "second conversion"; that is, a new and perhaps deeper appropriation of faith. Members who have been involved in the church for years, entering into its activities and organizations and yet still held fast by the old habits of life and thought, suddenly or gradually in the process of Bible study come to an experience of new illumination and great reality. There follows a quickening of commitment that marks a new stage in the pilgrimage of faith.

Nominal faith becomes a living reality upon which life finds its meaning.

Again, Bible study has the effect of bringing the biblical perspective to bear on the problems of daily life and sending men forth in mission. No one has suggested that Bible study guarantees this any more than a second conversion, but when men and women listen to scripture week in and week out they often discover that the Bible is indeed speaking to them at precisely the points of daily life, of business and money, of sex and family, of leisure and escape. They find it hard not to examine their concrete obedience in the world in the light of the covenant of God. People who have listened politely to sermons for years, when they gather together to listen to God's word from the Bible, are more likely to squirm in the face of honest confrontation, and only with difficulty can they brush aside the demands upon their lives.

Preaching

Preaching in the congregation is the way of covenant renewal. It is the proclamation of the gospel, new each time, that reminds men that they are called to be God's people, that relates them to their salvation history, and that provides directives for obedience where God has placed them in his world. In the inner city, where the Bible is being taken seriously, preaching is biblical through and through. The preacher defines his task as "breaking open" the word of God to the congregation. For preaching to have integrity, however, the congregation is required to be as fully involved as the preacher. The proclamation of the word depends not only upon the faithfulness of the minister, but also upon the corporate involvement of the whole people of God. When the members of a congregation are engaged in a continuing study of the Bible they also are able to enter into the preaching of the word as active participants in a dialogue. Preaching is a corporate act and demands participation. It is related to communion, for in the preaching of the word the minister is also called upon to explain and illuminate the meaning of the word enacted at the table.

Dialogue can become a reality when the congregation is involved in a pattern of weekly Bible study. Then the preacher is able to use the passage for the week as the scripture from which he preaches, speaking to a congregation many of whose members have already been wrestling with the passage and thinking about the issues and questions it raises. Together he and the congregation stand under the word of God, seeking to hear it afresh and live by its direction.

The dialogue of preaching and its vitality can be encouraged in many ways. One method is to involve laymen in the sermon preparation itself. In the East Harlem Protestant Parish the minister responsible for the Sunday sermon goes through this process. On Monday he studies the passage with his colleagues at a staff Bible study, seeking to acquire, with the help of all critical tools, the necessary professional preparation concerning the passage. On Wednesday at a noon staff lunch he outlines his sermon as he then sees it, accepting suggestions and picking up ideas and usually criticism. This provides for his colleagues, who will be in lay Bible study groups scattered through the parish that evening, some basis for focusing the group discussions. Often one or another of the groups will discuss what they think should be included in the sermon or what topics dealt with. On Thursday morning after eight-thirty worship, the preacher receives the reports of these groups and on the basis of them writes the final draft of his sermon. This process is not as complicated as it sounds and does bring a vitality to preaching that often engenders true dialogue between God and his people.

It is clear in Luther's writings that the congregation is to defend the scripture against the preacher.[1] They must be prepared to chal-

---

[1] See Luther, "The Right and Power of a Christian Congregation or Community to Judge All Teaching and to Call, Appoint and Dismiss Teachers," *Works of Martin Luther* (Philadelphia Edition), pp. 75-85. In some Lutheran liturgies today, at the time of the installation of the pastor, the congregation is explicitly charged with the task of defending the Word against the preacher.

lenge him if he does not preach the true and lively word. In the average congregation this is obviously an impossibility, for they do not know enough about the Bible to defend it. The normal pattern of reading the scripture some twenty minutes before the sermon, with hymns, offering, long prayer, and announcements in between, is also designed effectively to eliminate any possibility of the congregation's recognizing the connection between the scripture and the sermon. A good many clergy have been led to read the scripture and immediately to follow this by the preaching of the word. In some congregations the lectern has been done away with, or else the preacher picks up the Bible after reading the scripture and carries it to the pulpit, clearly symbolizing by his actions as well as by his words that his job is to read God's word and then expound it so that its relevance, truth, and power might be apprehended by all those present, including himself. Above all he will point to Jesus Christ and to the meaning of his life and death and resurrection.

Thus the integrity of preaching depends upon its becoming a corporate act of the congregation. The preacher must become a biblical preacher, with all that this involves. As Daniel Jenkins has rightly said, the minister must be a theologian. He is called upon to steer the ship and not to entertain the passengers. In this sense he must be a biblical scholar able to illuminate the Bible in language that will bring it alive for the men, women, and children of his congregation. This is, however, no more important than that the congregation itself be struggling to become biblically literate. This would suggest that a congregation not itself interested in understanding God's covenant in the Bible is not likely to catch fire no matter how impressive and empowered the preaching.

Issues
for Missionary Structures

In this and subsequent chapters the final section will recapitulate briefly the substance of the chapter and then deal with aspects of this material which need to be subjected to the criticism and insight of the first section of this study. In this chapter, for example, we must ask if our Bible study pattern is viable in the light of what we have said about the inner-city culture of today.

We have suggested in this chapter that Bible study as a normative aspect of corporate life is essential and basic to a missionary congregation. Only as the Bible becomes familiar territory and the biblical perspective natural will the lordship of Christ become a reality and God's covenant the foundation of the community of his people. Three major issues arise when this structure is affirmed as central.

Bible Study as a Normative
Activity of the Congregation

Is this a real possibility in the inner city? With this, as with every other demanding structure for the congregation, serious objections at once arise, and from many angles. First, are men and women willing and able to undertake such regular and disciplined study? Inner-city people, as we have seen in Chapter 1, are not naturally oriented nor accustomed to study of a reflective nature. They receive through visual means, and usually as spectators. The lectionary for inner-city parishes takes this into account by the simple device of a picture each week that seeks to illustrate the Bible passage. Corporate worship which involves participation and enlists all present in acting out the drama of salvation supports this understanding of Bible study. The most significant testimony comes from the parishes in a variety of inner city situations that report with considerable conviction that weekly Bible study, after some preliminary discouragement, has now become a regular and central part of the gathered life of the congregation. Where a congregation has continued to hold meetings week after week, even though only a few people came, they have usually found that gradually Bible study becomes a habit for a substantial portion of the congregation. In East Harlem recently one woman, making a nasty remark about the character of a parishioner, said, "She's nothing but a Wednesday-Sunday Christian." It is also the conviction of those involved that Bible study becomes exciting to people because of the enlivening presence of the Holy Spirit. The dynamics of such a Christian group may be analyzed helpfully by psychology, but the church also affirms that when men and women gather to study the Bible in Christ's name God grants them insight and illumination by his Spirit.

The second objection arises from ecclesiastical rigidity and denominational pressure. The moment Bible study becomes one of the basic foci of the gathered life of the congregation the traditional "table of organization" with its great variety of groups and activities is badly undercut. When the congregation is expected not only to attend worship faithfully on Sunday, but also to devote a whole block of time each week to Bible study, the other organizations are going to wither away, or better, will be largely abandoned, to the irritation of those in the denominational hierarchy who assume that no good church would be without a men's fellowship, women's society, missionary group, and all the rest. We suggest that the present predicament of the church demands that most of these groups be given up for the sake of mission. If the justification for the organization is fellowship, then God may grant that a far deeper understanding of fellowship will be discovered in the Bible study group. If the justification is an institutional function which must be fulfilled, let us examine whether that function needs in fact to be fulfilled at all. Where there are demands to maintain the congregation in its necessary institutional aspects it is likely that most of them can be met by asking one or another of the Bible study groups to take over the particular responsibility. If a church supper is planned one of the Bible study groups can take charge. The every-member canvass can be assigned to the Bible study groups, with each taking responsibility for calling on all the members in its sector of the parish, as it would be doing in any case.

Another obvious objection arises from the radical differences between the world of the Bible and the life of the modern city. How can we expect to get across the talk of lambs and vineyards and flowing streams to city children whose experience is limited to tenement streets and crowded subways? The Bible is laden with rural nostalgia and images. The answer at a superficial and yet significant level is given by Hollywood, for the average inner city child is likely to have seen most of the spectacular movies with biblical themes. Bible life and times via *The Ten Commandments, David and Bathsheba, The Robe,* and other such films are thoroughly familiar territory. At a more important level, the main archetypes in the Bible are somehow conveyed to men and women even if their own experience is distorted or limited. When the Bible speaks of God as a father the East Harlem child understands that something more is implied than he has discovered through his own family relationships. Above all, however, the Bible does introduce men in all times and places to a strange world that turns their values and their expectations upside down. Barth long ago reminded the Christians that when they turn to the Bible they do not find answers to their questions, but are confronted with God. Whatever experiences or understanding men bring, whether from a rural or industrial world, they are, in the Bible, led "into a new world, into the world of God."

In a recent urban consultation a denominational executive opened up this problem of the rural character of biblical imagery as a serious issue and suggested that perhaps new symbols were needed. To a man, the urban pastors present disagreed and affirmed the possibility of recovering and using with integrity the images of father, servant, shepherd, the words of Ps. 23, and the many parables of Jesus set in a seemingly different context. They felt that in confronting men with the world of the Bible these images were not an obstacle and were rather more useful than any new images or symbols that might be introduced.

Another objection arises out of the mobility, either real or expected, in urban life. How can any congregation talk about "long-range, consistent, continual" Bible study? This is perhaps a less serious problem in the inner city, where mobility is more a state of mind than a reality, than in suburbia where mobility brings a procession through a given church. One may also hope that a vital Christian community might act as a stabilizing force in a given situation, that it might be so meaningful to its people that their movement out would no longer seem either necessary or desirable. But mobility may also have certain positive results as we shall suggest below.

The Problem of Human Rigidity

We have noted that the initiation of Bible study may meet with resistance in a congregation. There is another kind of rigidity which is likely to be more serious. The flexibility and openness to change that is suggested in the concept of a living covenant, of a God who is presently active, of a word that is preached with relevance and demand and freshness in each situation, seems to contradict the customary congregational patterns, traditional, conservative, unchanging. People who want "to take your troubles to church this Sunday and leave them," as a familiar subway advertisement suggests, are not readily going to accept the idea that churchgoing, taken in light of mission, will be anything but restful. We affirm, however, that in Bible study there is a structure of congregational life that offers some possibility at least of exposing men and women to the active, demanding, judging, and redeeming Lord with whom, albeit unconsciously or accidentally, they have entered into a covenant relationship at their baptism or confirmation.

Another human expectation that falls under the heading of rigidity is the desire for clear-cut answers, for some definite authority that can be accepted or rejected, but usually may be taken for granted. Inner-city people come to the Bible looking for answers. It is jolting to learn that they are going to have to work, to enter into a biblical perspective, and that pat answers will never be found. Some will turn away in the shock of discovering that in this kind of study the Bible is not treated as a morality book.

Often they will find their way to other churches, Jehovah's Witnesses or other sect groups that provide the faithful with the security of categorical answers. Facts of human life lead men to seek this kind of escape from the contingency of existence and the reality of human life as one of choice and genuine freedom of decision in the context of obedience. In the Bible study pattern for a missionary congregation we argue for a method that requires personal involvement and the use of intelligence and brings the word into living dialogue with the world and with God's people.

The vital element here is that before the requirements of the Bible, love of God and love of neighbor, varieties of human gifts avail nothing. In the inner city, men and women of no formal education and/or limited intelligence, stand before God on the same level as those who have great erudition and intelligence. It is no easier for one than for the other to love and accept love. At the heart of human life, and in the task of Bible study, it is possible for all men to learn from one another as their human differences grow unimportant before God.

Church Order

Finally, we must ask if the concept of covenant begins to deal with the problem of institutionalism which so seriously hampers the mission of the congregation. As defined in Chapter 2, the issues centered in the tendency of local churches in our time to become ends in themselves, self-serving and introverted. In denial of the gospel the life of the congregation is designed to meet the needs of its members. In a missionary congregation, however, life is directed outward, bound in obedience to its Lord.

In seeking to begin with Bible study as normative, we suggest the need to face head-on the question of authority. In the Bible God is the initiator who makes a covenant with his people and then sustains them for the sake of mission. In a word, the form of church government can never be that of a democracy, for whether authority is vested in a clergyman, in a governing body such as vestry or session, or in the congregation as a whole, this authority is exercised in stewardship and not autonomously. Christ is king in the congregation. Genuine, continual Bible study designed to hear God's word as direct and relevant for today may serve as a reminder that the congregation and all it does is under God's direction, not that of the local governing body. There can be a great difference in attitude and concern between a vestry that meets to conduct the affairs of a human institution and one that meets to conduct the affairs of a human institution sustained by God and called to do his business of mission.

I have not attempted here to deal with all the issues relating to authority but only to affirm that in Bible study all denominations find at least part of the essential locus of the authority under which the congregation is called to live and work. Authority also involves variety, intricate and sometimes flexible relationships between biblical canon, historic creeds, doctrine of the ministry, and liturgy, depending upon one's religious heritage. Whatever the equation, however, finally at stake is the recognition that Christ is Lord, his authority supreme over men. This is a hard lesson for American Christians to learn, for they find the political imagery of king, lord, ruler, and even authority distasteful.

Another aspect of institutionalism to which we earlier called attention was the homogeneous, self-chosen character of so many congregations. They are congenial gatherings of like-minded people. These are natural human tendencies. Men find themselves gravitating toward congenial groups. They class themselves and others in social stratification. A congregation must fight back against these human tendencies. The Bible study pattern here does cut across something of the problem by seeking to start on a geographical basis, or sometimes on a vocational one, but not on the foundation of groups already formed by natural factors of homogeneity. Here is a built-in principle of renewal that cuts across social cliques and forces unity to emerge, if it comes at all, in the context of Bible study and life together in Christ.

Mobility, to the degree that it is not catastrophic in the changes

90

in a congregation, can also work to open the life of the self-chosen people. New people coming in must be met on their own terms. They are not so likely to take old patterns for granted. Further, it is an interesting discovery in some urban parishes that those who move out tend to be the church leaders. This requires the church to keep training new persons for leadership. While most clergy would look upon this as a mixed blessing, blessing it indeed may be. Even with children mobility can help keep open the reality that God's church is for everyone, and not only to serve those who are already in. Each summer one church in New York sets up a card table in the middle of the tenement blocks and projects, registering for Vacation Bible School new children, not already involved in the program. These children provide access to parents, bringing new traditions, different perspectives, and new demands into the ongoing life of the congregation. In this simple way a door of fervent renewal has been kept open.

So far, we have suggested that a missionary congregation meets to study the Bible as well as to worship. There are other patterns of adult study, some of which will be considered in Chapter 5, but the purpose in this chapter has been to give one concrete illustration of what is means to take seriously our first theological consensus in the light of modern urban life. This leads to the issue of church order. God's covenant means that the church, its facilities, and all it does is subject to God's will. God's authority must be recognized and expressed in any missionary congregation. This goes beyond Bible study, of course, but what is essential is the expression of the community's faith in the authority of its Lord.

5
WORSHIP
IN A
MISSIONARY
CONGREGATION

Jesus Christ is Lord, Lord of the church and Lord of the world. The Christian celebrates this reality in worship. Worship is the substance of the Christian life, for in this relationship the community that confesses that "Jesus Christ is Lord" expresses the meaning of his rulership. In meeting for corporate worship, Christians acknowledge the power and reality of God who is their creator, redeemer, and the source of their hope. In this context they search out God's word for them, are fed at the Lord's Table, and are encouraged to enter anew into their work in the world. In gathering for worship, they demonstrate by their unity the truth and power of Christ to overcome all human barriers.

To be human is to worship, to have an object of ultimate loyalty and devotion by which a man defines the meaning and purpose of his life. This is the uniqueness of being human, for no matter how unconscious in fact a man's ultimate loyalties may be or how various the idols he worships, he must find a meaning for his existence. For Christians to be truly human is to know that we are creatures called to give our praise, thanksgiving, and devotion to God who is our creator, and through Jesus Christ our redeemer and our hope. Worship in a congregation that gathers to acknowledge its Lord and seek his will and direction is thus supremely a political event. Christ's lordship is affirmed, his presence in the midst of the congregation is a reality, and in the unity of the people there is a foretaste of the kingdom of God. In this chapter we wish to suggest structures for worship that are emerging in the inner city, beginning with an examination of the integrity of the sacraments and then describing in some detail an inner-city liturgy. As the Bible study or other small group complements and prepares for corporate worship, so corporate worship brings together all the elements in a congregation to celebrate the gospel. In a mass society corporate worship can build upon, though transcend, the common experiences of men who live so fully in a corporate world. It will succeed when it calls men from the role of spectator to that of active participant.

An honest appraisal of most congregations at worship indicates how far removed are worship patterns from reflecting either corporate involvement or genuine encounter with a living Lord. Worship forms, unchanged in generations, no longer have power to lead men into the presence of God or call them forth from a spectator attitude. Instead of upholding before God on Sunday the concerns of daily life, the Sunday service becomes a religious rite, cut off from all relationship to the ordinary concerns of the world.

More significant, perhaps, is the fact that when most congregations gather for worship they deny, by their appearance, the very gospel they seek to affirm. They confess that Jesus Christ is Lord, but they reflect only a human community that does not witness to the New Testament description of the radically new human relationships made real in Christ. In the context of the early church human distinctions were abolished. There was neither male nor female, Greek nor Jew, bond nor free, but all were made one. This radical community, which cuts across all human need for partial communities in which we can set limits in terms of our involvement, was something new under the sun. Protestant churches by and large are simply a good example of a human community expressive of the natural needs all men have to be part of a group, but one in which they may set limits to their participation, define in non-biblical terms the character of those who are permitted to join, and use it to fulfill their own needs. It is of the nature of the Christian community when it gathers for worship that it be a place where the living presence of Christ is known and mediated and demonstrated. An authentic Christian community testifies to the presence of Christ in such a way that it stands in strong contradistinction to the many other forms of community where we also find meaning for our lives.

In the inner city the congregation which is a holdover from previous immigrant groups cannot escape the inconsistency between what it professes about the inclusiveness of the church and its own exclusiveness. The problem is even more poignant, however. The average church member, part of a homogeneous human family in the church, really has no experience whatever of the real joy and truth of the gospel. As long as human community is all he experiences, the power of Christ to reconcile human differences and make all men one is merely a kind of pious hope with almost no reality. As more and more is written about *koinonia* in its biblical and ideal meaning the more obvious is the judgment upon the present life of the ordinary congregation.

In the city there is a unique opportunity both to face the pre-

94

dicament and to take advantage of the opportunity for worship. Here, when the congregation is growing and alive, the clergy often find among their members a great variety of religious traditions. In one congregation there may be West Indian Negroes with an Anglican background, a substantial number of Baptists, Pentecostalists, Methodists, ex-Roman Catholics, and some others who have no previous church affiliation or experience. In such a context no traditional pattern of worship can be taken for granted. There is rather great freedom to seek forms of worship that provide vital and meaningful expressions of man's need to worship and give thanks to his God. Missionary congregations in the inner city have not settled for a lowest common denominator, but have sought worship forms that take tradition seriously and yet are alive in the world of today.

As one looks for patterns of worship in a missionary congregation, several initial assumptions are important. Worship is seen as the response to God. The initiative lies in his hands, for men are called first of all to respond to what he has done. In this way congregations seek to avoid the deadly dangers of passive worship. Again, worship involves the complete participation of men in the service. The word "liturgy" means work. Thus patterns of worship are sought which provide channels through which men may truly enter into acts of thanksgiving and praise, make real confessions that come from the heart, sing with joy, enter into the dialogue of preaching, and eat at a table where Christ is host. In almost all traditions one can find evidence of new stress upon congregational participation as essential to worship. Thus in a missionary congregation, along with Bible study, worship is becoming one of the two foci of the gathered life.

Communion

The climax of worship is the service of communion. Such was the testimony of the early church, when Christians gathered together primarily to break bread and drink wine in remembrance of the life and death and coming again of their Lord Jesus Christ. This was the emphasis of the reformers who gave the communion back to the people. John Calvin, who attempted to institute weekly communion in Geneva, affirmed that genuine worship demanded it. Today, wherever one glimpses signs in the church of renewal and vitality, it almost always follows that the sacrament of the Lord's Supper is central in the community of faith. This is true whether one speaks of the worker-priests in Paris, the Iona Community in Scotland, Taizé, the House Churches in Leeds, or of parishes in the United States. The main principles of communion, which are important in providing us with a basis for noting the present inadequacies of most congregational worship, have emerged as follows:

1. Communion should be normative in worship, a familiar and customary part of worship. Weekly communion may not be practical or essential for most congregations, but the liturgy can readily make clear that the Sunday-morning service is one of ante-communion. As the congregation begins to discover again that its life is nourished by the sacrament and is dependent upon Christ, the frequency of the Lord's Supper will increase, not as an imposition, but as an absolute necessity. Communion as a special service, held a few times a year, or for those who "like it," is simply wrong.

2. The communion table should be a central focus for the congregation. Instead of its being a problem (it is often an altar pushed back against the wall or tucked unobtrusively away under the pulpit until needed), the table should be a dominating feature in the architecture of the worship center. Early churches were designed to enable God's people to gather around the table, for it was not primarily at an altar but at a family table that the children of God came together to share in a feast. Different traditions may argue about the nomenclature. The name "altar-table" seems to do justice to most elements.

3. Communion is a corporate act involving a common action on the part of the whole gathered family of God. Instead of being an individual, private, personal action, communion must express

the family nature of the congregation. It is presently quite possible, whether people receive the elements in their seats or go forward to the rail, for them to engage in an act of individual piety and nothing more. True communion is an extended family, joyfully gathering together for a great festival in which all share deeply.

4. Communion, while filled with mystery, must be familiar and natural. When people do not really understand what they are doing communion can become something magical and almost superstitious, peculiar, special, and esoteric. The elements should be ordinary bread and wine, the actions natural and personal, and the participation joyful.

In the preceding chapter it was affirmed that the integrity of preaching depends upon the participation and understanding of the congregation. The integrity of communion also depends upon the congregation and its quality of life together. In breaking bread together Christians confess that in Jesus Christ they have been made into one family; they are now children of a common Father and subjects of one Lord. Integrity in communion would then seem to depend upon the congregation's being in reality a family and gathering with some common understanding of the act of worship in which they are engaged. Missionary structures are therefore required which enable this unity to be discovered, if God will grant it, and which express the style of a family.

It is too easy in our day for a congregation to be made up of virtual strangers, men and women whose lives do not touch outside the context of the morning worship. While the Christian affirms in faith that by commitment to Christ men are made into brothers, it is a subjective fact that this reality must be expressed by the quality of life together. A man's children are part of his family through no volition of their own, but it is imperative that the meaning of the given relationship find a concrete pattern by which they come to see and understand in action the meaning of brotherhood, fatherhood, and sonship. Without this the objective fact loses reality and meaning. So it is dangerous to speak of the objective reality of the Lord's Supper when those who gather have little to do with one another and do not in fact recognize the ultimate unity which has been given to them as members of the body of Christ.

Thus the first step in recovery of the integrity of communion is that the congregation discover in specific and real ways its unity. This is one reason why the small group movement has become such an important element in the life of the church. (See Chapter 6.) In this context one can come to know a brother in Christ and find the joy and meaning which this relationship makes possible. Then on Sunday morning when God's people gather around the table they know each other as brothers and feel themselves a family which gathers together to receive the bread and wine. Increasingly in churches the communion table is being placed in a central position so that the congregation can gather to receive the sacrament in a circle around it, either altogether or in groups. The experience of corporateness becomes real in worship when a participant not only listens to the minister's words—"All you who do truly and earnestly repent of your sins, are in love and charity with your neighbor, and intend to lead a new life following the commandments of God"—but also comes forward around the table to look into the faces of his brothers against whom he has sinned or for whom he feels enmity. Often the words take on a new depth and urgency. Now he is not permitted the luxury of individual communion. Now he is part of a body in which he recognizes in a much more threatening way his own involvement, his own sin, his own need, and ultimately, his own joy in participation.

The integrity of communion depends also upon those who participate having some understanding of what they are doing. It needs to be a familiar and well-known action, veiled as its ultimate meaning may still be in the mystery of God's presence. In the inner city the learning process usually starts from the beginning. With so many different traditions, coupled with the normal Christian ignorance, the East Harlem Protestant Parish has found that the best place to begin is to re-enact the service of holy communion in a way that will dramatize for people what is happening in every service.

Maundy Thursday offered such an opportunity. In a sanctuary seating about three hundred the pews were taken up in order to make way for long tables across the front half of the church. One hundred and fifty or more people could then gather in the sanctuary for a fellowship meal just as Jesus gathered in the upper room for the Last Supper with his disciples. The meal began about eight o'clock with the congregation sitting at the tables which had been spread with big loaves of Italian bread, jugs of wine, and platters of sardines, symbolic of the connection between the feeding of the five thousand and the elements of the Lord's Supper. During the meal people spontaneously led in the singing of hymns, and there was a general time of fellowship together. Following the meal the minister stood in front of the large communion table which dominated the chancel of the church and preached briefly on the servanthood of the disciples, using as his text the passage from the Last Supper where Jesus insisted on washing his disciples' feet. Here was the reminder that the only authority the Christian has is that of the servant, even as Christ refused any other authority. The minister spoke of the reason why he wore a stole, derived from the Latin word for towel and now a reminder of the towel with which Jesus girded himself and washed the feet of his disciples at the last supper. Following the sermon the minister went to the bottom steps of the chancel. In groups of eight those who had gathered at the tables came and stood facing him on the steps. Kneeling down he wiped the toes of their shoes with a rag which had been sewn into the end of his stole—again a vivid reminder of the nature of his ministry and a re-enactment of the act of Jesus with his disciples. When this foot-washing service had been completed the people brought a loaf of bread and the wine remaining from the meal at the tables and placed it on the communion table as the whole congregation gathered around in three large circles. Then the ordinary bread of the supper was broken and the wine was poured out. The elements were passed from hand to hand as at the Last Supper. When everyone had received the bread they all ate together just as a family might partake together when all had been served. Likewise everyone drank together as a further symbol of their unity. While the elements were being passed, a communion hymn was sung. Following the communion benediction and a service of Tenebrae in which the Lenten candles were put out, the congregation went out in the darkness to wait for Good Friday.

I have described the service at some length as a way of indicating how a congregation can be helped to re-enact in as full a way as possible the service of holy communion. In this way the normal service of communion might take on a new depth and meaning as they recognize how the two are intimately related. Thus on an ordinary communion Sunday the whole congregation will be invited to receive the elements while standing around the table. The bread and wine which are used are brought from home by one of the members as their offering and placed on the back table at the beginning of the service. Then when the offering is received at the beginning of the service of Holy Communion the bread and wine and money will be brought forward together by the elders or deacons and placed upon the communion table, with one of the elders offering the prayer on behalf of the whole congregation. Again the bread should be an ordinary loaf, perhaps a loaf of French bread that people customarily like to eat in an inner-city neighborhood. During the consecration of the elements, at the point of the fraction, the bread will be broken and during the receiving of communion the pieces passed from hand to hand as people pass the bread in a family. The elements, the offering, the gathering around the table—all of these are designed to remind the congregation that this is a family feast. In this natural setting men re-enact once again, as a mighty event, the whole story of their salvation in the death and resurrection of Jesus Christ. At the same time, gathered around the table, they remember the first Lord's Supper and its initiation by Christ and then, faced with the task of obedience in the world, look forward to the coming of Christ with hope.

It is all these things—that is to say, the whole meaning of the faith —which is gathered up in the service of communion.

Pastors who have experimented with this kind of worship indicate that communion has come to hold a central place in the life of their church. Experiment, of course, is a poor word. This is not experimentation but recovery of authentic patterns of worship which closely parallel the life of the New Testament Church and would have brought joy to the heart of the reformers. In many inner-city parishes communion is now being celebrated each Sunday at an early service, though this is a poor solution, and once a month in the regular service and on every other possible occasion during the year. It is simply a fact that even the people in the congregation who do not go regularly to church try to be present on communion Sunday.

We have argued that the integrity of communion, insofar as it depends upon men, is related to the quality of life in the congregation. It must see itself as a family united by a common Lord. It must understand what is happening when the members gather at the table in a central act of faith and obedience. No structures of worship can produce integrity, nor can men take the initiative in true worship away from God. But a missionary congregation, dependent upon God's faithfulness, will be sustained as it gathers at his table.

Baptism

Baptism is also a political event. It points to the lordship of Christ and marks a person's entrance into the promises of the covenant of God. In the case of believer's baptism, and provisionally in the case of infant baptism, it means the acceptance of a new relationship of obedience. Markus Barth, for one, now is giving great emphasis to baptism as nothing less than the rite of ordination by which the Christian is set apart for the full-time service of his Lord. In every Protestant tradition, whatever the form and time of baptism, the service itself is a once and for all sign of a man's incorporation into the body of Christ.

There is no consensus on some important theological issues relating to baptism, but the obvious differences here are not crucial for this consideration of missionary structures. For a missionary congregation, seeking in worship to express its obedience to its Lord, the important element is the integrity with which a particular congregation performs baptisms, whatever the particular position it holds on infant versus believer baptism. Baptism in each case marks a decisive boundary line between the community called to mission and the world in which it is called to witness and service. It is a serious act of commitment to be entered into with understanding. Baptism must not lapse into some kind of cultic practice or superstitious rite designed to protect infants, but must continue to mark the promise of new life given in Christ and the call to discipleship.

For inner-city congregations the crucial issue for the integrity of baptism, whatever the denomination, centers in the common affirmation that baptism is the sign of new life in Christ. In this sacrament men die to their old lives through their real or symbolic washing in the water and are born again in the power of Jesus Christ. The assumption and claim is nothing less than that in Christ men do indeed enter into a new life, no longer trapped by their sinfulness, but enabled by grace to live as sons of God. These are bold affirmations, rooted in the New Testament but often denied by the churches of today, threatened by cultural captivity. They presume a congregation that is seeking to live by grace and though still sinful (justified yet still sinful) reflects a style of life which points to its Lord. The integrity of baptism depends in part on a congregation that is concerned to reflect this gift of new life and which contains a body of men and women for whom baptism is an abiding reality. It makes no sense to perform the service if the person thus baptized is not brought into a congregation in which there are saints seeking in their daily lives to bear witness to the reality of the new life in Christ through their obedience to him. When baptism is not done with the expectation that the old has been put off and the new has begun, it is a denial of the gospel. One expression of this expectation, a continuing concern with the habits of the Christian life, will be considered in the following chapter. They provide the discipline through which the reality of the new life in Christ may find expression.

When a congregation contains men and women who have been born again—that is, baptized into Christ—and whose daily obedience is one of dependence upon his grace, then baptism becomes an important sacrament in the life of the family of God. Then those who are baptized, whether infants, children, or adults, become surrounded with all kinds of relatives who are concerned about their nurture. The Christian name, given at baptism, becomes a mark of loyalty and vocation in Christ's army.

For the congregations in the inner city which do practice infant baptism, there are two further areas with which they must be concerned in their missionary structures. First, the church has no business engaging in private baptisms. Baptism as the sign of God's grace given to the church is not an individual matter. It marks the child's entrance into the body of Christ and thus is an act of the whole body. Increasingly congregations are affirming that baptism must be performed as part of a regular service of worship at which the congregation is present and may take its proper part in the liturgy. The Anglican Ernest Southcott in *Receive This Child* affirms this point categorically and indicates how in the life of his parish in Leeds, England, corporate baptisms were a vital part of the missionary witness of the congregation. In the new Presbyterian (U.S.A.) order of worship there is a strong insistence that baptisms be part of a regular service of worship and not private affairs.

In the second place, inner city congregations must struggle with a serious tension that arises when a child is presented for baptism where there is little assurance that he will be brought up in the context of the community of faith. Perhaps the parents are not members and only seek to please a grandmother. The witness of the church to its Lord is seen to be badly blunted by promiscuous baptism. Some policy decision is often developed that makes clear the seriousness with which the congregation performs baptism. In this way the clergy are given the support necessary to make any pattern workable. The use of godparents who can be responsible sponsors sometimes provides one way out of the dilemma. Another clue lies in the possibility of requiring substantial discussion with parents before any baptism, often providing an opportunity for genuine evangelistic encounter. The minister who superficially denies a child the rite of baptism or who too easily accedes to a request in either case may be missing a unique opportunity for witness to the parents.

One final question related to baptism affects all congregations. This has to do with the age at which children are either baptized as believers or taken into membership. There has been a considerable tendency in recent years to push up the age which children join the church, often waiting until the high-school years. Several inner-city congregations have suggested an intriguing alternative by lowering the age to the junior level, fourth to sixth grade. At this time children may become communicant members, but later on, as older teen-agers or young adults, must enter into a course that prepares for adult membership. This additional stage serves as a reminder that the Christian life is a pilgrimage in which study and learning are always necessary. The junior children are keenly interested in religious matters, able to be stimulated and excited by biblical material, and keenly concerned to be permitted to come to the family table. They thus are old enough to come to the table and receive the gifts of bread and wine, but not yet expected to share fully in all the family councils and decisions.

The Understanding of Worship

The patterns of worship in a missionary congregation must reflect the nature of the gathered community. We have begun with a discussion of the two sacraments, for in a particular way they point to the Lord of the church. Baptism proclaims the entrance into the new relationship, and communion witnesses to the continuing renewal of the promise thus made. Now we turn to the full service of worship which must also be an expression of the relationship of the congregation to the Lord of its life.

The freedom and necessity of the inner city provide for a combination of a rich liturgical framework—that is to say, responses, confessions, prayers—with a very informal mood and spirit with room for freedom and change. It is much easier to evolve liturgical worship when there are varieties of traditions present so that no one can say, "You always do it this way." When a congregation has this freedom, then not only does congregational participation become greatly prized, but one discovers that worship patterns often develop in the direction of many of the historic liturgies and thus make possible a unity among different traditions.

The service of worship to be described here as a suggestion for a missionary congregation was developed in the East Harlem Protestant Parish. It takes as its guiding principle the word "participation." The whole congregation was asked to be caught up and involved in a common action that expressed both feelings and intellect. Participation meant to *recall* in worship the mighty acts of God so that they would become again the personal history of those present. The use of the church year provided the obvious framework through which to celebrate the events that were important. Advent, for example, came to be the time when the congregation entered into the longing of Israel for its Messiah.

Participation meant also to *re-enact* these salvation events so that they became living realities, contemporary and compelling. Earlier we described how one congregation re-enacts the Last Supper on Maundy Thursday. Palm Sunday was celebrated with a dialogue sermon that described vividly the feelings of various groups on that day leading into Holy Week. The service ended not just with passing out palms, but with the whole congregation joining in a procession and shouting their hosannas. All the important events of the church year can find their own form of re-enactment.

Participation meant also to *await* the fulfillment of God's promises in Christ. The worship of the church sought to point ahead to the time when its Lord will return. It knows that what has already begun must be completed. It lives between the times.

Forms of worship are no guarantee of the presence of the Holy Spirit. But in seeking to discover patterns that open the participants to the possibility of worship, that point in the right direction, that make it hard to remain uninvolved or indifferent, congregations enter into a necessary task. If worship is to be an open channel of God's grace it must be understood by those who enter into the liturgy, and they must accept their active role. The service described below also was developed in the light of the current emphasis on the gathered and dispersed life of the church. Sunday worship by the community was seen as the gathering of Christ's soldiers from their various places of service along the world's battlefronts. The movement of the service reflects this metaphor.

Reporting

As the people gather in the sanctuary of the church they give thanks in hymns and words of praise for their safe return and for the continual care and protection of God. Then comes the confession, said by all the people, a confession in part of the very real sins and transgressions of the week past. Following the kyrie and the prayer for pardon the whole congregation joins in the twenty-third Psalm or other appropriate scripture used as words of assurance.

Then the minister comes down from the chancel and, standing in the midst of the people, asks them what is happening to them in God's world. This is called the "concerns of the church" and is more than a fancy name for announcements. A man stands and tells about an important meeting for parents at the school; another asks help in getting signatures on a petition for police protection; a woman urges us all to register so we can vote. There are reports by name of those sick and in trouble. Others ask that all pray for an occasion of joy, the recovery of health, return of a loved one, or perhaps a wedding anniversary. Then, informed by the people, the minister returns to the table and, kneeling down, prays for the very specific issues which his people are confronting in their life as Christians in the world, for their needs and fears, as well as for issues other than those of which he has just been informed.

God's Word

The second major movement of the service involves the scripture and sermon, the point at which the congregation listens again to God's word and seeks to accept his direction in their lives. The Old Testament lesson for the week is read, followed by a Psalm, and then the New Testament passage. Directly following this reading the minister carries the Bible to the pulpit and enters into the sermon, hoping that the clear relation between the word of scripture and the sermon will be made apparent. The preaching in the parish is biblical, throughout the year related directly to the exposition and application of the scripture passage that will have been studied during the preceding week by all the Bible study groups. With this kind of preparation for preaching on the part of the laity, the sermon can again become a genuine dialogue, with both preacher and congregation wrestling with God's word to them and standing under its judgment and encouragement. Like soldiers called back from the front lines, they are given perspective and order for their work of witness and service amid the principalities and powers of this world.

Communion

Communion is now celebrated about twice a month in the worship life of the full congregation, but every service emphasizes its character as ante-communion. The offertory on the Sundays without communion is a reminder of this fact. In addition, each Sunday there is a service of Holy Communion at eight-thirty.

The communion service used in this congregation was described earlier. Here we would only add that the service begins with an act of fellowship, derived from the kiss of peace. The congregation shake one another's hands as all sing an appropriate hymn. Then the elements, which were placed on a table near the door before the service, are brought forward along with the offering of money. One of the elders, on behalf of the congregation, gives the offertory prayer. As much of the symbolism as possible is that of a family festival when all the relatives gather for a big celebration. Here God's people re-enact the whole drama of their salvation, are united again to Christ and to one another, and are given the food of life that they might enter again into God's work.

Return

At the conclusion of the service the congregation repeats the Parish Purpose, based on the words which Jesus read in the synagogue:

The Spirit of the Lord is upon me because he hath anointed me to preach the Gospel to the poor. He hath sent me to heal the broken-hearted, to preach deliverance to the captives and recovering of sight to the blind, to set at liberty those that are oppressed, to proclaim a year when men may find acceptance with the Lord. Amen.

In this way the people are reminded that they gather together in worship in order to lift up to God their life in the world and then, fed by word and sacrament, to return to the world as the locus of their obedience. This servant passage emphasizes again that in the world the only authority of the Christian is that of the servant and that service is the task to which God calls. The benediction also strengthens men in this purpose:

Go forth into the world in peace; be of good courage; hold fast that which is good; render to no man evil for evil; strengthen the fainthearted; support the weak, help the afflicted; honor all men; love and serve the Lord, rejoicing in the power of the Holy Spirit. And the blessing of God Almighty, the Father, the Son, and the Holy Spirit, be upon you, and remain with you for ever. Amen.

Issues
for Missionary Structures

In a paradoxical fashion, worship is both the substance of life for the Christian, for which he draws apart from the world and joins with his brothers in a celebration of the gospel, and also a place where the church must confront the world. If man must worship, then modern men who enter into the church and encounter it at worship should see there enacted the truth of the gospel. We submit that authentic Christian worship describes an experience in the uniqueness of which the stranger or inquirer will sense a new reality that transcends ordinary community and idolatrous forms of worship. Modern man is frantic for something worth his worship. In Christian worship missionary congregations seek to lead him through word and sacrament to an encounter with the true God. This is not at all to suggest that encounter leads to conversion. Rejection is always, in man's freedom, a possible response. In a missionary congregation the patterns of worship are called upon only to enable a genuine confrontation and express the truth of what Christian life is all about.

Living worship is vital and alive not only because it re-enacts the truth for men, but also because the primary archetypal experiences of human existence—birth, marriage, family, death—are expressed. The church still is involved for most men in the rites of passage, but in a missionary congregation these must be truly a witness to the gospel and not tribal customs. For example, baptisms must never be private or family affairs. Marriages are to be celebrated as part of a service of congregational worship, perhaps at a special time, but in the context of corporate worship. Funerals are the occasion when, in the presence often of many non-Christians, the church is called upon, not primarily for a eulogy of the dead, but for a living confession of the faith of the church. In these ways the missionary congregation can begin to fill the void in human life left meaningless without ritual or authentic worship.

In worship the church must also meet the need for man in mass society, man who often has to experience a sense of belonging to a mass that matters, to feel the exhilaration of being with brothers in a community that is purposeful and vital. This is why mass man can contribute to Christian worship at its best, for he stands, not in a world of private experiences and individual worship, but has found meaningful experiences in the corporate context of union, political party, or factory floor. Structurally, one implication is that churches should not be too large. Better a small sanctuary full than a large one with twice the number present. This may seem a small point, but as we turn in the next chapter to consider the need for men to find their places in small groups, we must put alongside this the equally important need to be part of a movement that calls them out of themselves and gives to life a vibrant sense of direction—a God to worship and a cause for which to venture.

A missionary congregation needs to have provisions for renewal of worship. These structures can be built into the life of a congregation as suggested earlier by such a simple device as rearranging the furniture of the sanctuary. The lectionary described earlier has a worship liturgy for the season in the front that allows new ideas of worship to be introduced from time to time. In many inner-city congregations a dialogue sermon has provided a stimulating and sometimes disconcerting change of pace in worship. Again, this is not to experiment or "play around" with worship, but to seek ways in which worship remains open to God's grace, a channel of renewal for the life of the congregation.

Any discussion of authentic worship at once confronts the disagreeable reality of present church architecture. The very design and purpose of most of our buildings thwart in part the effort to develop missionary structures. In new church design the missionary purpose of the congregation must be central. From our general discussion of worship several conclusions relating to church architecture can be drawn:

1. The pulpit, the table, and the font need to be clearly related, without any one dominating the sanctuary. The divided chancel is wrong; the table pushed back as an altar is wrong; the font buried in a corner is wrong. The artistic problem of relating all

three is great but must be given serious attention, whatever the initial architecture of the sanctuary. The best clue comes in the suggestion that as in a living room, attention can move from one center to another, from the fireplace to the picture window, to the table, et cetera.

2. The action of the minister should move at times on the level of the congregation. In particular, the actions at the Lord's table must be among the people, not above and beyond. He should thus be the representative of the congregation at times as well as God's spokesman to it.

3. The choir belongs as part of the congregation, leading it in the praise of God and not, gayly decked out, somewhere up in front as a part of the entertainment. Many a congregation has discovered that its singing improved greatly when the choir joined the congregation, sitting in front or side pews as part of the family.

Perhaps the most serious issues raised by this chapter lie in quite another direction. They involve the necessity of the congregation's drawing some kind of boundary around its gathered life in terms of membership procedures. These are touchy problems that always lead to controversy and often to ill feeling. Regardless of this, it is important to affirm the necessity for a missionary congregation to wrestle soberly with these matters. In Chapter 3 we indicated how casually the church today often takes the matter of membership. Integrity of baptism means that church membership must be a matter of ultimate significance both for the believer and for the congregation. The Church of the Saviour in Washington, D. C., provides a vivid illustration of a congregation that has taken this matter seriously. The story of the rich young ruler in Matt. 19:16-22 offers another helpful guide. The key principle that should govern every effort to arrive at a viable policy on membership is not that of exclusiveness or self-preservation, but that of mission. In order to serve Christ in that particular situation, what requirements are necessary for those who join in order that they will become, not members of an organization, but participants in Christ's mission?

111

In the matter of communion the same principle is important. The centrality of communion will be diluted and perhaps lost if those participating in it are not part of Christ's family. But to fence the table is not somehow to protect Christ, but to enable his servants to draw apart in order that they might be sent again on mission. Without the right kind of protection the gathered life cannot provide refreshment and renewal. The early church dismissed the catecumens before communion. A missionary congregation must ask itself what policy, in its situation, will serve the same purpose and forward the missionary work of Christ.

6
THE
STYLE OF
LIFE IN THE
CONGREGATION

Does the missionary congregation today have a distinctive life that marks its off from the secular communities of its time? This question focuses the concern of this chapter. In every period of church history there have emerged these distinctive patterns of life which made it clear to the world that Christ's followers were marked men. The political vocation of God's people has time and again led the church to define its obedience in unmistakable fashion. The varied and changing patterns that have expressed the Christian life are often these days referred to as "a style of life" for the church. In our day, when the church and culture are so intertwined and Christians no longer stand out in any distinguishable way from their contemporaries, the search for an appropriate style of life has become an urgent matter. The salt must recover its flavor, the leaven its power to ferment. A missionary congregation must ask what it must be and do to reflect its obedience to Christ. In the inner city the question is raised at once, precisely because a congregation that does not express some uniqueness of life is lost amid indifference and apathy.

On the Meaning of "Style"

The search for a style of life in the past has often led in the direction of sectarianism. In order to separate themselves from the evil world Christians have frequently moved out of the world into a kind of religious ghetto where they have sought to live a Christian life in isolation from the evil world. This temptation, which in a curious way now besets much of American Protestantism, must be rejected. Our search is for a style of life that enables the congregation to live fully in the world. In this chapter we will consider what structures are necessary in the gathered life of the congregation in order that members may grow in their true humanity as the people of God and dare to live as men in this world.

Our search for a style of life in our day will not focus primarily on a new piety, however, but on preparation for witness and service in a world which has rejected God. A fine phrase often used to describe a style of life for our day is "holy worldliness." We can readily understand what is meant by "holy otherworldliness" or "unholy worldliness." We expect the church to live in one of two different worlds and like to keep them honestly separated. The style of life for the church in the twentieth century involves learning once again to live a holy life in the midst of the world. The missionary congregation is called so to live that it is able to dirty its hands in the life of the world where God is at work and at the same time to share in the joyous liberty of Christian freedom. Dietrich Bonhoeffer in his prison letters has spoken of the meaning of Christian worldliness.

During the last year or so I have come to appreciate the "worldliness" of Christianity as never before. The Christian is not *homo religiosus*, but a man, pure and simple, just as Jesus was man, compared with John the Baptist anyhow. I don't mean the shallow this-worldliness of the enlightened, of the busy, the comfortable or the lascivious. It's something much more profound than that, something in which the knowledge of death and resurrection is ever present. I believe Luther lived a this-worldly life in this sense. . . . It is only by living completely in this world that one learns to believe.[1]

The predicament of the congregation today arises when joining the church and participating in its life does not really presuppose or elicit a serious decision to commit one's full obedience to Christ and to accept the gifts of a new Lord, a new family, and a new vocation. In traditional terms, we do not expect conversion.

Conversion has largely become old fashioned, or where it is still spoken about it becomes stereotyped and conventional. The New Testament belief that when a man was gripped by the power of Christ, he entered into a completely new pattern of life that demanded of him discipline and obedience, has given way to nominal membership. In our day membership in the average church demands no real change in habits and patterns of life. It is often a relationship that can be readily added to previous commitments and patterns without any real change being necessary. In fact, church membership is the calling to sainthood, but not many congregations expect saints to emerge from their midst these days. Perhaps this is why congregational life so continually looks back to Christ and to the early church as its pattern, when it should in fact be looking around to discover Christ as a present reality, breaking forth in

[1] *Prisoner for God,* pp. 168-69. Used by permission of The Macmillan Company and Student Christian Movement Press, publishers of the British edition, *Letters and Papers from Prison.*

power in human lives in this place and that place. Christ is here and at work. Men are called to enter into his task as a present reality, not as a memory of a past reality.

The reality of conversion must become the starting point for a style of life, for this style is only a means to give expression to a man's confession of faith in Christ and his commitment to serve him. Whether one begins with believer's baptism or confirmation, a man's personal response to Christ and acceptance of the new life to which he is called marks the beginning of a whole new set of relationships which a style of life is only designed to nourish and sustain. Conversion is primarily the relationship of love to Christ and to neighbor. As Luther once suggested, until he is saved, a man inescapably is preoccupied with himself and looks at the world through his own eyes. When a man is justified by faith, is accepted by Christ, then he has nothing better to do than return this love, "to be a Christ to his neighbor." A style of life is designed to enable these relationships of love to grow and to sustain a man in the life-long pilgrimage of faith. The Christian is always on the way, never someone who has reached the goal. Paul addressed the members of the churches as "saints," not because they had achieved some kind of goodness, but because they had committed their lives to Christ and were struggling to live in this new relationship. He could not take the depth of their commitment for granted, but he could pray that they might more and more learn to live by grace alone. This is what sustains the Christian in his new loyalty.

In terms of missionary structures, the primary focus of this chapter is on the small cellular units in a congregation within which nurture and training may take place and style emerge. We shall here apply this structure to three aspects of our life in Christ on the assumption that true commitment will be sustained only as we express our obedience in relationship to our new Lord (habits of the Christian life), to our new family (life together), and to our new vocation (equipment for service). In each case regular, small group meetings seem to offer the only effective method of development. Thus we begin to describe the gathered life of the church as centering around two foci: Corporate worship and cellular units. The small group as the context for Bible study has already been introduced, but here its centrality for a style of life also will be obvious.

The Elements of a Style of Life

We come to a specific consideration of the patterns for a style of life. It is crucial to recognize the contingent quality of any such effort, for a style of life is always changing, useful for the particular situation, but always in danger of becoming rigid or Pharisaical unless its purpose is kept firmly in mind. It is to express the new life of God's people and enable them to enter into God's missionary task in their own time and place. The world, as fully as the gospel, determines the appropriate style for a particular congregation. The suggestions given here may be primarily useful in making clear the importance of a style of life and in offering some lines of advance that will enable those in other situations to find their own solutions.

New Lord: *Training in the Habits of the Christian Life*

When Christ becomes the Lord of a man's life that person enters into a never-completed training process that teaches him to express the reality of this new relationship. Traditionally the church has spoken of this under the heading of discipline. In our day this word has such unpleasant connotations that a number of congregations prefer the word "habit." Habits of thinking, feeling, and responding appropriate to the Christian life must replace the old habits with which men come into the church at their conversion. In *The Screwtape Letters* C. S. Lewis described the efforts of the old tempter to console his nephew who had just lost a victim to the enemy (the church). He reminds the young tempter that the intended victim is not yet lost, for all his old habits are still in their possession. Unless they

117

are changed the man will soon fall away from Christ, and they can claim him again.

New Christians fool themselves badly when they expect that all their old patterns of life will be displaced by the fervor of their new commitment. Only by the long-term work of building new habits in the place of the old can they hope to be sustained in a pattern of life which will express the freedom which only habit makes possible. Only when men have learned to make the many small decisions of life that reflect their obedience to Christ out of habit are they able to exercise genuine freedom in the larger issues for which no habit is adequate.

Habits of the Christian life serve two basic purposes. In the first place, they teach men to use the channels of grace. The habit of Bible study or of regular corporate worship is an example. By making such activities natural and customary men open their lives to God. When men learn to pray, for example, and it becomes a habit, they go on praying when they do not at all feel like it; that is, when they are most nearly cut off from God and most need to pray. No habit can ever guarantee that men will be open to God, but it can help keep the possibility open. Health habits do not guarantee good health, but without them poor health is far more likely. These vertical habits are similar for all Christians.

In the second place, the habits of the Christian are part of his preparation for service to Christ. Just as a soldier must be broken of many civilian habits and brought under the rigorous discipline of the army in order that in battle he may respond instinctively and naturally, so the Christian recruit must be trained in the discipline of his new calling. This implies that these habits of the Christian life are never fixed or universal, but always tentative, for the present situation, subject to change in the light of the particular sector of the battlefront to which the troops will be deployed. In other words, a missionary congregation will seek the habits of the Christian life as an essential part of its life, but the specific content will vary from one situation to another. The church that takes discipline seriously almost always faces, sooner or later, a severe problem of legalism, for each particular form of the habits is likely to take on a rigidity that is used to judge men rather than equip them.

Here and there congregations have begun to wrestle with habits for their life in Christ. In *Call to Commitment* Elizabeth O'Connor described the significant witness in this regard by the Church of the Saviour in Washington, D. C. One typical pattern is the following from St. Stephen's Church in Houston, Texas:

As an expression of my love for God I will:

1. Seek God's plan through a daily time of listening prayer and Bible reading.

2. Worship weekly in the Church with emphasis on Holy Communion.

3. Participate regularly in weekly faith study and prayer fellowship.

4. Give regularly a definite grateful share of my income to the spread of God's kingdom through the Church and in the world.

And as an expression of love for my neighbor, I will:

5. Pray daily for others with thanksgiving.

6. Exercise faithfully my particular ministry in the fellowship of the Church.

7. Witness by word and deed in the world to the love of God in Christ as I have come to know it. *So help me God.*

This pattern from St. Stephen's Church would hardly be considered very demanding or extensive, but in fact few congregations these days make any attempt in this direction at all. Part of the reason lies in the reaction to the legalism and rigidity of American Protestantism in an earlier day that placed too much emphasis upon superficial adherence to discipline. More basic, I suspect, is the secularism of the congregation, which means that religious virtues expressed in the life open to grace are not so important as institutional competence and other values simply translated from the secular realm into the gathered life of the church. It takes no special discipline for a banker to serve as church treasurer. Also

119

discipline, either corporate or self-imposed, is not very congenial to American life with its "other-directed" character.

In order to attack the problems in the way of developing habits of the Christian life the small group has become an essential instrument. In this setting newer members may be encouraged to begin the task of learning new habits with the encouragement and example of older members. More important, parishes that have struggled with the recovery of a style of life all bear witness to the need for the sustaining, chastening, and encouraging help of brothers in a small group if the habits are to be developed and maintained. Mutual commitment to prayer, for example, is far more likely to lead men and women to pray regularly than the most determined self-discipline.

In this discussion we have made heavy use of the military metaphor, for it expresses the character of our new life. In Christ men enter into his warfare. This is the pathway of true humanity. One final implication of the metaphor is an important reminder to the church. The situation of the army of Christ is always that of wartime. No civilian role is possible. Even off the military reservation the professional soldier is on duty, in uniform, unlike the peacetime man who performs military duty on the army base and then dons civilian clothes off the post. "No soldier on service gets entangled in civilian pursuits, since his aim is to satisfy the one who enlisted him" (II Tim. 2:4). The habits of the Christian life enable the soldier of Christ to live both in the gathered and dispersed life of the congregation equipped by the training that makes obedience possible.

New Family:
Life Together in the Church

The second aspect of a style of life involves the discovery of the gift of life together in unity, which is both the gift of the gospel and part of the gospel itself. Men are given a *new family*. In a world where depersonalization is

120

an ever-present reality men and women need to see and experience a community of love and reconciliation if they are to appropriate the gift of new life in the gospel. The style of life for the Christian, then, will involve participation in the life of a congregation where he shares in the experience of unity in Christ and is sustained in his new humanity. In the context of community life concerned with personal relationships of love and trust the individual may become a true person again.

A new structure of congregational life is called for which makes provision for genuine meeting between persons, a context in which the masks of self-deception and distrust will be maintained only with difficulty and in which men and women will begin to relate to each other at the level of their true humanity in Christ. When the congregation in our day meets primarily on Sunday morning, whether in a little storefront church in the inner city or in a large city church, it is almost certainly as strangers to one another that most people gather.

The secret of success in a family comes from learning to live with one another so that there is understanding and mutual commitment. Mutual dependence, unity, and love—these are the marks of a community gathered in Christ. They are gifts of Christ to his people, but they must be open to receive and enjoy them. The style of life is a preparation for and reception of Christ's gift. Essentially, some form of cellular life provides the opportunity for genuine meeting, for the full sharing in the experiences for which God calls us together, to learn to bear one another's burdens and to speak the truth in love. These are the qualities of a style of life for the congregation.

The missionary congregation, then, will make basic provision for its members to meet in small groups, not as a sidelight or an option for those who like it, but as a normative part of its life. Such groups are often called "house churches," for in their life together they engage in a full expression of the life of the church. Acts 2:42 provides the basic pattern:

1. Apostles teaching (Bible study)
2. Fellowship (true sharing)
3. Breaking of bread (communion and worship)
4. Prayers (intercession)

The important thing to note is that each of these elements involves an objective task. In the small group there is work to be done. The Bible must be studied, with an eye to its relevance and meaning for obedience in the world; prayers must be offered for the real needs of men; and the group must join in worship and study. The point is crucial, for at the moment the churches are much involved everywhere in developing the "small group" in a way that is destined to disillusionment or failure. When a group is organized for "spiritual growth" or "fellowship" or mutual encouragement, these are objectives that come only as a gift of God and not through the efforts of men. They are desirable by-products, but so subjectively oriented as to lead only to impossible expectations when they are the immediate object of the small group meeting. When men meet to study the Bible because they are biblically illiterate they may expect to be rewarded through hard work and application with some success. In the process they may rejoice also in the gift of unity, mutual love, and encouragement. Their purpose was an objective one whose accomplishment was within their power. The context, however, made possible the discovery of their entrance into a true family of faith.

To say it again, small groups are essential for a missionary congregation. They may be organized in a wide variety of ways—vocational groups; geographically; for study in a particular area, at the church or in homes. But their purpose must be defined in objective terms that involve work to be done and goals to be achieved. When this is clearly set forth and understood, we may proceed to pray for God's gift of our new family to emerge in the process of our small-group involvement. Briefly, we seek at least the following relationships to be discovered and to grow in our life together.

Unity in Christ: The Meaning of "Koinonia." The church is a community of love where the personal presence of Jesus Christ is known and where his love masters the community and builds it into a genuine unity. In our world of many human fellowships it is almost impossible to capture with any impact the biblical word *koinonia* which is translated by "fellowship." There is a radical difference between the human fellowship which men seek in a multiplicity of human communities and that of which the Bible speaks. As human beings men are driven to seek community; it is part of their very nature. Normal human communities are characterized by a clearly defined restriction on membership, by a definite limitation on the commitment required of its members, and by demands which are quite explicit and acceptable to those who join. In God's church men are called to go beyond this and to find intimate community with people who are incredibly different, with whom they have no natural human homogeneity, and whom they usually would have no other occasion to know. In the Letter to the Romans, Paul wrote: "For as in one body we have many members, and all the members do not have the same function, so we, though many, are one body in Christ, and individually members one of another." (12:4-5.)

The point being made again and again is that the Christian community is not one among a number of other communities, but something more is involved in its nature. It must be the bedrock on which the meaning of other loyalties and commitments is founded. It is to reflect a unity that transcends all human differences and demonstrates in the midst of the world the reality of reconciliation. There is a poignant tone in the many recent descriptions of *koinonia* in such ideal and wonderful terms, precisely because the authors are so fully aware that such expressions of *koinonia* are hardly to be found. The fact that the church as a true family of God receives so much attention does serve to judge present actions and may lead to a new openness in the future. In a broken, strife-ridden world where one group wars against another people need to believe that community between human beings is possible. When the church gathers into its life like-minded people with many homogeneous factors in their background and tradition it really denies them the possibility of the kind of experience of *koinonia* which God offers to his people.

In the inner-city churches of our day, where all the heterogeneity of men finds expression and where church attendance is not part of a cultural expectation, there is a desperate need to express *koinonia* and a unique opportunity to discover its meaning. Nothing else can readily bring men together. Only if men find their point of common identity in Christ do they have anything in common.

Openness to All Men. The first major battle of the early church had to do with the admission to membership of non-Jews. Did a person have to become a Jew first; that is to say, to enter into a religious, racial, and national community as a first step in commitment to Christ? The answer was an emphatic "no." Christians really believe "there is neither Jew nor Greek, there is neither slave nor free, there is neither male nor female; for you are all one in Christ Jesus" (Gal. 3:28). Participation in the life of the church was open directly to *any human being willing to accept Jesus Christ as Lord.* Perhaps the ambiguity of the situation today lies in this: that the other gods which compete for men's loyalty do not object to their entering into the life of the church, introverted as it is. Whereas in the faith of the early church the Roman gods and the other secular loyalties saw Christ for what he was, a rival god that threatened their existence. To accept Christ was to deny human idolatries and enter into an army in conflict with them.

There is an ambiguous character, however, about entrance into the life of the church. In a sense Christians are *volunteers* who of their own choice submit to a military discipline. Yet anyone who has entered this army knows also that he was a *draftee,* that it was by God's choice that he was selected and it was Christ who claimed him. This paradox points to a fact about the life of the church. It is Christ himself who is the center of the church, and nothing must be allowed to obscure this reality, to stand in his way, to set him aside, or to subordinate him to another interest or end, even momentarily.

Bearing One Another's Burdens. A missionary congregation depends upon the mutual ministries of all members of the family. As Eph. 4:1-16 stresses emphatically, the strength of the whole body grows only when each member is working properly; that is, accepts his gift from the Holy Spirit and exercises it for the sake of all. In a family, bearing each other's burdens is an almost unconscious expression of mutual love and concern. In a congregation the small group makes it possible for the members to discover love, to feel concern, and to bear one another's burdens. This is the reality that Protestantism calls the priesthood of all believers. In coming to know each other the congregation can discover in its midst those who have pastoral and other gifts needful for the common life, thus relieving the clergyman of the full task of "burden-bearing" and enabling him to give attention to his legitimate function of locating and training the variety of gifts which are given to a congregation.

Speaking the Truth in Love. In a family brothers speak the truth in love. This necessary family relationship is relevant also for a missionary congregation. "Speaking the truth in love, we are to grow up in every way into him who is the head, into Christ." (Eph. 4:15.) Without this gift, the congregation remains a collection of individuals, determined to avoid conflict and maintain pleasant but largely innocuous relationships. In the small group experience, there is hope that men may learn to speak the truth in love, for this prevents "burden-bearing" from becoming sentimental or paternalistic. It means also that real issues can be considered, for though there is disagreement, and even bitterness, a family can endure. The experience of many congregations today testifies to the new health and vigor that has emerged when the members began, often slowly and with hesitation, to speak the truth in the growing context of mutual love.

Both parts of the statement "to speak the truth in love" are equally important. One without the other becomes a source of mistrust, confusion, and ultimate disunity. Together they point to the heart of true humanity, the ability to love and the freedom to live honestly before all men. These gifts men learn to use in the church are precisely the expressions of true humanity the world so badly needs to see demonstrated in its midst. When men learn to love one another they may also learn to love the world.

New Life: *Equipping the Saints for Life in Dispersion*

The present search for a style of life has led directly to the vocation of Christians in the world. This is the locus of their obedience. Use of the word "vocation" need not cause confusion if we see that the point is to emphasize the Christian calling as a soldier of Christ. However he may work to earn his living, whatever his secular vocation and avocations, his basic calling is set by his new life in Christ. Obedience to the Lord is now his central task in life, all the time and everywhere.

Just as we have suggested how the congregation in worship can provide a setting in which to reflect upon and prepare for life in dispersion, so small group participation is a complementary task. Here is provided the kind of study and preparation which deals with the specific problems and concrete issues of obedience where men must earn their living, play, reside, and all the rest.

In this view the church in its gathered life serves as something like a boot camp or training base before the troops are sent up to the front lines, a place of preparation. In the world, in life in dispersion, the energy of Christians in their secular occupations must reflect the spirit of their Lord; they must enter into the struggle against the principalities and powers of evil and minister with compassion and love to those in need. Here is an attempt to face the false antithesis between the world and the church and to remind congregations that in accepting Christ as Lord their calling is for a purpose. The church exists for mission, not primarily for the service of its members.

"By definition *the Christian is one who stands in the midst of the*

126

world to minister to the world. He is one who seeks, beyond all else, to be an instrument of the redemptive mission of the worldly God." [2] A man's conversion is real only if it turns him back into the world, able now to live with eyes of faith. This implies that life in the church must deal with the concrete issues of obedience in the world. The family of the church must be the active source of one's fighting weapons for involvement in the world. These are strong demands, but there is no short cut. "The creation of this new and revolutionary Christian atmosphere depends on the common efforts of each and every Christian. . . . Every man has his own little world to influence, to change, to Christianize. That is what we must do as united individuals." [3]

Small groups in a congregation are providing one way of structuring this preparation for the Christian's life in the world. The Bible study method outlined in Chapter 4 as well as the house church described in the preceding section are always seeking to relate the attention of their members to the issues of obedience they face in the world. It is also possible to organize small groups concerned primarily with considering the specific tasks which members face in the world. The study-group program of the Montview Presbyterian Church in Denver brought together members with a common arena of involvement in the world. Thus doctors, for example, would meet regularly at a very early morning hour to look squarely at the tensions they faced as Christians in their professional life.

Such an emphasis in a local congregation can now be encouraged and deepened by the denominational concern expressed through a number of well-run conferences for laymen of various professions and types of employment. In recent years the American Baptist Convention in a series of conferences at Green Lake, Wisconsin, has broken important ground in this direction. Following in part the pattern of the European Evangelical Academy, men of one profession are brought together with theologians for a no-holds-barred

[2] *The Church and Its Changing Ministry*, p. 11.
[3] Abbé Michonneau, *Revolution in a City Parish*, p. 100.

127

consideration of the meaning of obedience for that group of laymen. In the years ahead local communities, through councils of churches and lay centers, will also give a good deal of attention to this area. Since few congregations are large enough to organize along occupational lines, some such interdenominational co-operation seems imperative.

The small group structure oriented to vocational obedience for a local congregation implies study that is not focused on deepening the members' spiritual life, or even on gaining information, but on their work in the world and the kind of understanding and support they need to be effective. The Church of the Saviour in Washington, D. C., has been the best-known and most forceful example of this structure for a congregation. Its members are expected to give one evening each week in an intensive study program designed to equip them for their witness in the world. Equally important, for those who wish to join the congregation there is a program involving at least two years of hard, disciplined study that precedes their membership.

Occupation is only one possible focus for small groups, for in our day the lives of Christians intersect with the world at other points that are often of great significance. For inner-city workers leisure time may be a far more important point of obedience than employment. Thus equipping the saints must involve not only occupational issues, but must also prepare them for their role in community organizations and in politics and for their leisure time activities. In considering the role of the congregation in all these four important areas laymen are likely to discover that traditional differences used to align the activities of the members—sex and age especially—no longer have much importance. Creative obedience in leisure, community life, and politics are common tasks in which each must learn from others. Members working in parent's groups or tenant's associations might find these interests the basis for study and life together for a time. This also suggests that a missionary congregation not only will seek to equip its members for their place of witness and service, but may even enter into a conscious attempt at planned dispersion in order to infiltrate a variety of the world's activities. This point will be considered further in the next chapter.

In conclusion, the task of equipping the saints for their new life in the world demands participation in a group that is willing to deal seriously with specific issues and tensions without trying to hand out ready-made or pat answers. Men and women need to be allowed with all honesty to face up to themselves and to their world. This is part of being truly human.

Issues
for Missionary Structures

This chapter has indicated the important areas in which congregations are working as they seek to discover a style of life that will express their relationship to their Lord. The habits of the Christian life reflect the fact of a new Lord whose rule provides direction and purpose for a man's life; the entrance into a new family provides the context in which to discover the full meaning of humanity and find sustaining relationships; and attention to the specific problems of obedience and service in the world serves to equip the laity for their new lifework. In all these the basic missionary structure is that of the small group. Now we must begin this concluding section by asking whether such a pattern is a real possibility and about any inherent dangers and problems. Then we shall turn more briefly to implications that arise from the specific sections of the chapter.

The Small Group as a Basic Structure

The primary problem is simply institutional inertia, but it arises from two sides. On the one hand, the demoninational hierarchy sometimes objects to any pattern which departs radically from the expected table of church organization. On the other hand, individual congregations are slow to change,

129

particularly when the small group almost certainly demands a heightened degree of personal involvement and commitment.

Here and there the necessary breakthrough has occurred, and congregations have established this bifocal structure. In Little Rock, before accepting his call as pastor, Richard Hardie asked the session to consider such a pattern. The proposal was accepted and for over eleven years now has been the basis for the life of the congregation. In a number of inner-city parishes the need for a style of life in the midst of the frustration of mission made the congregation eager to try anything that offered some hope. The Bible study pattern described in Chapter 4 was one development, though the clergy from a variety of parishes report that it was two years or more until the new pattern became firmly established and Wednesday night Bible study was as much a part of the gathered life of the congregation as church on Sunday morning. The first six months to a year is often so discouraging that the effort is almost abandoned, but once the pattern is established it becomes easier to maintain. In other situations the breakthrough to a new pattern has come by a retreat for the church officers at one of the fine lay centers— Kirkridge, Parishfield, the Faith and Life Community, and many others. Here, in a neutral setting, under the direction of able and dedicated men who stand outside the immediate life of the congregational group, the officers can be challenged to the core about the mission of the church and the work of ministry. An interesting issue of the *Union Seminary Quarterly Review* was devoted to articles on renewal in situations other than inner city.[4] In every case the process was slow and difficult, but possible. The key was the necessity of some pattern of small groups as an integral aspect of the gathered life.

There are a variety of forms in which small groups may be organized—Bible study, house churches, vocational or study groups, prayer meetings, witnessing fellowships, and others. The constituent elements may vary somewhat, but an objective point of meet-

[4] XVI, No. 3 (March, 1961).

ing is necessary. Experience in many places suggests that such meetings must be both normative for a congregation and regular. The moment they become the possession of a pious few they are likely to lose momentum. This is not to suggest that a majority of the congregation will necessarily participate, but it does mean that the expected pattern for the congregation, shared in by the responsible leadership, does focus on small groups. The important point is that the small unit be seen, not as a temporary expedient or special form, but as an essential structure of congregational life in our day. Only through this form will discipline be developed, true meeting between Christians take place, and men be equipped for witness and service in the world.

Small groups, like any other structure, however, do not guarantee renewal or vitality. They may afford a new possibility of faithfulness, but they easily become ends in themselves or fall into other dangers. There are several tests against which the life of the group may be judged.

1. Issues of fundamental importance in life in dispersion are discussed. This means real issues, not smoking and drinking, but the issues people want to evade—for doctors, medical care for the aged; for teachers, unionization.

2. As free as possible from ideology so that issues can be faced honestly and without more distortion than is inevitable. Professional groups, for example, need to be challenged by material other than from their own organizations.

3. The group seeks to act together or at least to arrive at a consensus.

4. The group backs up the person who does act in accordance with the claims of obedience. That is, the group takes seriously its solidarity.

All four of these tests underlie the fact that small groups are for mission and not primarily for purposes of personal religious growth. A pamphlet of the World Student Christian Federation summarizes this position:

A test of the validity of church life as *ekklesia* (its worship, church activities, and church organizations) is the extent to which this phase of being the Church prepares and nourishes the people of God for its other phase of being the Church, namely, its function as the salt when scattered in the world.

Such a criterion as this might well be used by a congregation in determining which of its present organizations may be permitted to wither away or be stopped at once.

Boundary Lines

The emphasis of this chapter upon discovering and maintaining the new humanity of the Christian raises again the question of church discipline, particularly in regard to membership. The role of the official church governing bodies can be with the necessary boundaries which mark off the gathered life of the church from its life in dispersion. This implies that church membership must become a matter of utter seriousness, whether through the severe pattern of the Church of the Saviour, with its study discipline and evidence of personal growth, or some pattern appropriate for the inner city that makes clear the decisive character of entrance into the family of Christ. In every situation the point is to be sure that those who enter the life of the church have the kind of relationship with Jesus Christ, at least in a preliminary form, which sustains them. The church must not preach forgiveness without taking repentance seriously. It must not baptize without church discipline. There must be no communion without confession.

This suggests that the congregation must maintain a paradoxical relationship to the world. On the one hand, it must establish its concern for the parish around it, for its own community. God always expects the congregation to care for more people than it is reaching. On the other hand:

God seeks men and women who will love him with all their heart and with all their soul and with all their mind and with all their strength;

therefore, no local church can be satisfied with some minimum of acceptance of the gospel message. God seeks those who will resist the dominion of sin to the point of the shedding of blood. This is why we are always seeking to intensify the commitment of our members, to draw together a core group of people who truly understand what it means to be the people of God, to remind ourselves as well as the world that we are a church. The truth to which a whole host of sects on the left wing of the Reformation and the various evangelical movements in American Protestantism are faithful when they made a serious call for commitment and sought to limit the fellowship of the church to those who made a commitment is now being acknowledged by inner city churches as they seek to know their true membership. God expects our faith to cost something, and he is continually asking more than any of us is willing to give.

What we are seeking may well be the abolition of "sect" and "church" as Troeltsch has described them for here in the inner city we are seeking the "sectarian church" and the "churchly sect." Both come to the same practical conclusion about their membership and their responsibility. The parish is as broad as God's concern, yet it is as narrow as his demand.[5]

The Small Group
and the Habits of the Christian Life

In this chapter we have discussed discipline under the rubrics of the habits of the Christian life, but traditionally discipline has involved the responsibility of the body to deal with members who break trust, engage in immorality, and otherwise violate the body of Christ. The Pharisaical and sometimes demonic misuse of the power to discipline in the past has made most ruling bodies reluctant to exercise any discipline whatsoever. Habits as described here are seen as a positive attempt to undergird the Christian. The problem of discipline or habits seems to be an essential element in a missionary congregation and cannot be simply ignored.

Here we have seen that the discipline needed to develop habits of the Christian life is primarily a function of the small group. In

[5] George Younger, speech, "The Church at Work in God's World."

this context men may take the steps of common commitment which provides for each the encouragement, chastening, and direction of others without the threat of the authority of church officers behind it. In a sense, one must accept voluntarily the pattern of discipline agreed upon in the group, but once accepted it must be taken with complete seriousness.

The genius of the small group in our inner-city world comes precisely when it is able to remain open to all men, when there are sufficient saints in the group so that without hesitation the misfit, the alcoholic, the Black Muslim, can be accepted in its midst. Only the leaven of a committed nucleus can sustain such a disparate fellowship, but when they are present, the miracle of acceptance and mutual love may be demonstrated. Whatever discipline Christians find necessary for their style of life, it always remains true that toward the world—to the sinner, the distraught, and the unlovable people of God's world—the congregation remains open, accepting, and, by God's grace, loving.

The Small Group
as the Extended Family

In the world men live in broken communities, including their families. The congregation is called to live as a true family, thus providing for men an image of what a human family might be, even amid the pressures of the inner city. Is this indeed a possibility in the church? We hold that the beginning of family life will come in face-to-face encounter made possible in small groups that cut across natural lines and bring men together with only the common denominator, Christ. Within the congregation there is the possibility of the variety of human life —old and young; rich and poor; Negro, white, and Puerto Rican; all sorts and conditions of men—that emasculated family life no longer makes possible. In the small group the anonymity of life can be broken. Here is a context in which apathy and discouragement can be broken through by the vitality of human relationships.

This points to the healing relationships in a family. The life of a congregation in certain periods of history has been marked by special gifts of healing. This was true of the New Testament church and seems usually to occur in new churches still in the flush of first generation religious enthusiasm. At such times the power of the Holy Spirit for direct healing appears most powerfully at work. Pentecostal groups today seem frequently blessed with such gifts. In the inner-city congregations, however, while such dramatic evidence of the Holy Spirit may be granted, more likely healing and changed lives will be the work of less sudden and more gradual process. For example, anomie is a kind of sickness for which healing is devoutly needed, but it cannot be dealt with by any frontal attack. Normlessness cannot be met by the appeal to moral standards. Persons caught by anomie can only be loved out of themselves, the vacuum filled with meaning that is truly a resurrection from living death. In a congregation that is becoming a family there is set free this power to love those who are loveless and unlovable. In the inner city life comes back in this slow process that involves testing, rejection, and new testing. The drug addict, hating himself, alone, defeated, will not easily believe that anyone can love him. But in the context of a community that does love him and does accept him, because he is the object of Christ's love, the process of healing may take place.

In concluding this chapter we would note that the expert in group dynamics is likely to be critical of the rather unprofessional manner in which small groups are permitted to operate in a missionary congregation. Any such meeting of people sets loose the interplay of human dynamics in ways that may be dangerous or destructive. This is a valid objection and points to a reality that will surely be encountered by any congregation that attempts this bifocal pattern. A domineering personality who tries to take over a group, a circle that turns introspective, personality conflicts—such problems are not to be pushed aside. Three defenses can be achieved by the groups against these dangers. First, the small group must have an objective task to which it is called so that "group therapy," under whatever guise, is not its raison d'être. Without this focus the chances of trouble are greatly enhanced, for then the success of the group depends upon the dynamics of human interaction pure and simple. In the second place, the task of the clergy or of members of the congregation must be precisely to become experts in the leadership of such groups. We have already suggested that in some situations the clergy's role will be to train the leaders of Bible study groups which will include not only diligent study of the Bible but insight into the dynamics that exist whenever people meet for any purpose. The matter is not put to rest. It will continue to arise in the ensuing discussion. Finally, the Christian affirms that when such groups meet in Christ's name, the Holy Spirit is present, informing, directing, and uniting the group.

7
THE
MINISTRY
OF THE
LAITY

Bible study, worship, and a developing style of life are all in part a preparation for the dispersion of the laity into the world. The world outside the church is the place where they must engage day by day in Christ's work of making and keeping men truly human, confront the principalities and powers of evil, and be sustained by their ultimate trust in the gospel. The congregation, of course, also faces the world corporately and as a body shares in Christ's missionary work. These corporate structures of mission will be taken up in the next chapter.

Here we seek to define patterns which will enable laymen to live and work with a Christian self-consciousness in the world.

The basic clue for missionary structures at this point lies in seeking as laity to follow the pattern of Christ's own engagement in the world: Incarnation (presence as a true man in the world), Crucifixion (ministry to the human needs of the world), and Resurrection (witness to the ultimate power and victory of God over the world). These are only different aspects of the one reality of witness and service to which Christ calls all his people, but we shall take them up under these three headings in order to deal with them in some kind of logical order.

We enter now into a realm of missionary concern in which the ordinary congregation is not very much at home. The old separation between the life of the church and the life of the world has usually been too strong. More important, the great new interest in the laity has in many cases simply turned inward, galvanizing men and women into vigorous work to support and maintain the congregation in its internal, institutional life. The time and devotion which many able and consecrated laymen devote to institutional aspects of church life is remarkable; it may also in the end of the day have been a tragic diversion from the work of Christ.

The Reality of the Incarnation

In the theological consensus we have underlined the need for the Christian to live in the world as a man, sharing fully in the situation where he finds himself, identified with the world, even as he maintains a loyalty that transcends it. As Christ entered into human flesh, so the Christian must be at home in the world, not in some hidden way, not on a raid to "take scalps," but going "native in all things save faith and morals," in Auden's fine phrase. We are talking about a self-conscious presence in the world as a Christian man, not better or different from other men, but present on Christ's business and able to understand the world through eyes of faith. Such a relation-

138

ship is possible because the Christian sees the whole world as the arena in which God is at work. This strange and startling idea that emerged in our theological consensus makes no sense unless the believer is immersed in the biblical record of God's activity. It makes of him a lay theologian, for the task of theology is the very human effort to understand the divine activity. It is the positive identification of the work of God in the life of the world, in the life of the church, and in the life of the believer. It means, for example, to read the morning newspaper to see what God is doing in his world.

To take the incarnation seriously in the ordering of the laity involves four interrelated aspects.

1. First of all is the task of *being truly present in the world*. If God is at work in the world, then the laity must join fully in the life of the world and in that context discover what they are called to do. Too often, eager Christians have insisted in the world that they brought to the situation ready-made answers to the complex problems of society. The Christian, when he shares in the true life of the world, in its loneliness and separation and distress, will then be able with some integrity to ask how his faith sheds light on the real problems and gives direction to their solution.

When the middle class, mostly white, theologically trained clergy of the East Harlem Protestant Parish began their work in the inner city they were baffled by the problem of how to communicate their faith to the people of the neighborhood. An able researcher was hired to help them overcome the barriers to communication. After some months they got an unexpected answer from their researcher. They were told in no uncertain terms that their own inability to live as men in the situation was the problem. They were in East Harlem as professionals, all-wise, observing, dissecting, and analyzing the life of the community, standing on the bank watching the flooding life of East Harlem sweep by, stiff with the resolve to do good and be Christian, but utterly unwilling to jump in, to share as men in the tumultuous life of those to whom they wished to minister. They had to learn what it means

139

to take the incarnation seriously, to share in East Harlem as citizens, tenants, parents, and in the context of these normal human relationships to discover that barriers of communication began to dissolve. To put it another way, the Christian is not a lifeguard standing on the bank of a river throwing life rings out to drowning men, while he himself is safely on the shore. He is also swept along by the flooding currents of life, fully involved in the common life of men but able to put his arm around another drowning man and point to Christ who saved them both.

Laymen are already present in the world. The problem is to provoke them to self-conscious acceptance of this fact and to take the consequences. They must see the public realm, the world of community—politics, work, and economics—as the locus of Christian living. To retreat into a private world for one's ultimate meaning in life, to find it only in home and family, is to cease to be a man. A person becomes truly human only as he enters into the public realm as well. There are two ways to destroy the humanity of a man, deny him privacy or block him from political action. Sometimes in an inner-city parish it is necessary to disperse laity consciously into various community groups to insure the presence of the church.

In the East Harlem Protestant Parish one simple structure that awoke people to a new awareness of their presence in the world was a door seal. The parish stumbled on this by accident. On many of the apartment and tenement doors in the community appeared a large door sticker from the local Roman Catholic parish that said in English and Spanish, "This is a Catholic home; propaganda of other religions not permitted." Annoyed by this negative Christian witness, the Protestant church members decided to respond in a more positive way. A door sticker about six inches square was designed with a symbol of clasped hands; the name of the church was written at the bottom and across the top the words in English and Spanish, "Welcome in the name of Christ." These door seals were then put on the outside of the homes of all the members scattered through the various projects and tenements of the community. What had begun simply as a reaction to the Roman Catholic negativism turned out to have much more drastic implications. Suddenly the door stickers said to the world that each of the homes where those stickers were found was a part of the church, a home where God's people lived, as rightly called part of the church as the big brick building on the corner. In this very important symbolic way the church was suddenly present not in one location in the community but in a hundred.

2. The Christians in dispersion must *engage in dialogue.* To be present in the world where God is at work suggests also in particular to engage in dialogue, now to learn to listen to the world as well as to speak, to discover from the world the meaning of its pain and the nature of its longing, not to produce ready-made answers to all the world's problems. The Detroit Industrial Mission is an immensely significant program of the church in dispersion which defines its task in large part as seeking to listen and understand what is happening in the Detroit industrial complex. Listen to the words of one of the staff of the mission:

> Those who are seriously concerned to live as Christians in their place of work struggle along with very little support from their pastor or other church members. They need expert, full-time help in order to discover for themselves the meaning of the Christian faith for the life and operation of industry. . . .
>
> Only by patiently concentrating on a few people in a few areas of industrial life could the D. I. M. staff earn the confidence it needed. It had to demonstrate that it really was interested in industrial problems with all their baffling complexities, and that it was more ready to share in concern than to produce slick solutions.

Another effort is marked by the beginnings of lay institutes in this country, designed in part, of course, for the training of laymen in their mission in the world, but which also provide a setting in which the church in the world can begin to enter into an honest dialogue. The pattern comes from the evangelical academies in Europe, where, ever since the end of the Second World War, recognizing its irrelevance to the problems of the whole of the reconstruction of the German nation, the church found a setting in which secular people were willing to discuss the concrete issues which were involved in their political, economic, and social lives. Here the church could expect no favorable audience but would gain a hearing only as the Christians present in a conference spoke a word of relevance. In this country lack of confrontation between the church and the world makes the dialogue more difficult. Christians do not really know how to enter into the kind of conversation that emerges often in the German experience. We can only suggest that the church and those who witness for Jesus Christ must be willing to enter into dialogue with the world; they must break away from the fatal monologue that emerges from the self-satisfied church. Many of the urgent problems of metropolitan life earlier considered reflect the fundamental breakdown of communication between elements in urban life. In entering into dialogue with their sectors of the world the laity seeks a reopening of communication within God's people and within the world. Now the focus is upon understanding in the world in order to serve the world. The question is not what the world is doing to the church and its institution, but rather where and how we are called to witness, to serve, and to minister. Service, not survival, is our only standard.

I first understood something of the necessity and meaning of this attitude of listening from the Rev. John Gensel, a Lutheran pastor in New York City who has been released half time from his regular parish responsibilities to become a pastor to jazz musicians. His new parish is the jazz spots of the city and the musicians who are involved. In a sensitive and appreciative manner Pastor Gensel has come to know these men and women, listened to them play, sat alongside of them, entered into their lives. As they have come to accept him as a person the effect upon him has been quite striking. With great appreciation, he speaks of the insight into the meaning of life they have given him—these sensitive, often brilliantly gifted musicians—through their awareness of the pain of segregation, of alienation and meaninglessness in modern life, their struggle for integrity. In this kind of listening to the world Pastor Gensel has also had to see with fresh eyes the meaning of the gospel. Although this illustration is of a clergyman, it can serve to dramatize what listening involves and point the way to the dialogue task of all Christians in the world.

When a new public housing project is opened, the East Harlem Protestant Parish at once seeks to move some of its members into the buildings as tenants. They can at once become outposts of the church. More important, they are able to organize a tenant's council and thus meet the other new residents in terms of their common need to develop in the project a pattern of authentic community. The congregation thus does not attack the project from outside, but through presence, participation, and listening joins in the life of the new community as men with other men.

3. The church in the world must *live with compassion*. As the church enters into God's world, learning to listen, it may also feel and care. The gift of love is the ultimate measure of the Christian life. One may pity the victims of injustice or even fight for justice with great energy, but it is another matter altogether to feel compassion for the victims of injustice, for they are so often unlovely people, quite uncongenial to our way of life, hardly people with whom we wish to become friends. There is no ministry in Christ's name without love, however: the kind of love with which Christ entered into the deep relationships of life, sometimes with the ordinary people of his day, but especially with the social misfits and outcasts.

This is to speak against the moralism of the churches who say, in effect, to the world, "Come and be like us. Then you are welcome." This kind of attitude, standing in judgment against the world, often distorts the mission of the churches. It is also to speak against the assumption that men live by bread alone, that is to say, against the willingness of Christians to give to good causes, to seek secular solutions to social problems, but not themselves to enter into the pain and anguish of involvement. To be a Good Samaritan is personally inconvenient; it interrupts plans and upsets schedules. Any inner-city pastor subject to the support of more prosperous congregations knows from sad experience how often utterly demanding and inconsiderate are those who as more privileged Christians want to help those in the slums. When the wealthy society women of Paris came to help Vincent de Paul they were shocked at the indifference and lack of appreciation from the poor. He counseled them, "You should not be shocked that they do not appreciate your good deeds, but grateful if they do not hate you." The drug addict does not want a keeper; he seeks a brother who is willing to enter into his pain and suffering with compassion. This will arise in the heart of a Christian as a gift of God, but only as he stands beside his brother.

4. *See with eyes of faith* (this is the task of reflection). In Chapter 3 the phrase "the secular wisdom of the gospel" was used. This is a way of saying that the Christian has been given a key to the meaning of history, to the life and destiny of men. Paul wrote: "For he has made known to us in all wisdom and insight the mystery of his will, according to his purpose which he set forth in Christ as a plan for the fullness of time, to unite all things in him, things in heaven and things on earth" (Eph. 1:9-10). To the church has been given a foretaste of the kingdom of God and a sure hope for the world. The missionary congregation is called to face, with utter realism, the mess of the world, the inhumanity of man, the seeming hopelessness of a divided world, and yet to live with confidence.

Here is involved a task of reflection as Christians seek to comprehend the new world of the metropolis and to understand how God is working through the new structures they see emerging. If the laity begins to engage in serious conversation with the spheres of public life, then they must be helped in this reflection by theological specialists. This is not a congenial task for activistic Americans, but as Christians are involved self-consciously in the world through presence, dialogue, and compassion, they inevitably seek understanding. In this search for meaning the clergy are a theological resource, chaplains to the laity in the task of theological reflection.

Nothing can be more central in the gathered life of Christians, wherever they meet, than the effort to discover the meaning of metropolitan life and the form and task of the church in the public sphere.

The Reality of the Crucifixion

Having begun to live as Christians in the world and to discover signs of Christ's work in the world, the congregation in dispersion is called to join him in his task, to enter into the redeeming enterprise in which he is engaged. In speaking of joining in Christ's task of making and keeping men truly human we shall consider three areas, overlapping often to be sure, but sufficiently distinct to remind us of the variety of human relationships and commitments—the world of work, of home, of community. What does it imply for missionary structures to serve Christ in these areas, to live in the way of the cross?

The World of Daily Work

Much of the outpouring of literature about Christianity and daily work is irrelevant or impractical. Christian faith, obedience to Christ in every situation, does indeed have drastic implications for the way in which men enter into their daily work. It does not mean, however, the kind of piety contained in the phrase "applying faith to daily work" which leads to the emphasis on prayer and devotion. The end result is congressional prayer breakfasts in Washington, not much more than a cultic ritual, unrelated in fact either to Christian faith or obedience in the world. This pattern denies the presence of God at work in the world; it divides the sacred and the secular again and implies that a God who is somewhere else must be connected with the world.

The other customary direction in considering the meaning of daily work is a moralistic one. This is "making the gospel relevant to secular work" by insisting on heroic service or more ethical

145

conduct by Christians. Fortunately, there are too many ethically sensitive persons outside the Christian fold to permit men to cherish any illusions here. In daily work the meaning of obedience is not primarily a matter of relating an ethical system—the gospel—to something else—the world of work. The difference, if any, between Christians and non-Christians in daily work does not lie at this point.

To take both God and the world seriously suggests that the starting point for a missionary understanding of daily work is simply the obedient response to Christ's gift of new life. He has made men new (justification by faith is the traditional doctrine) and thus daily work, whatever it may be, has meaning because God accepts it as an expression of man's faithful response to his lordship over all of life. The alternative to moralism and piety is contained in the phrase from Bonhoeffer referred to earlier—"holy worldliness." To be quite specific, this call to obedience by still sinful men in a sinful world might mean:

1. The willingness of the Christian to accept his work, no longer as a curse, but as the locus of his obedience. This is not to cross out all the questions of jobs a Christian cannot rightly enter into or the possibility of changing jobs. These are important, and in freedom men must make decisions in these areas. Here we only affirm that in earning their daily bread men are called to perform their task with faithfulness.

2. His willingness to live by grace; that is, not driven in any situation to try to excel others nor to be more moral or more honest, but as best one can, seeking only to do God's will through the power of the Holy Spirit. The Christian recognizes fully the ethical dilemmas, the gray shades of decision, and faces with honesty the difficulty of decision making and yet takes the risk involved in responsible life. This is to live in the recognition that the work of the world is carried on in imperfect terms. Faith in God's redeeming love can resolve the impossible tension between high ethical idealism and the practical necessity of life in community.

146

3. Willingness to take the job seriously on its own terms, good or bad, as the locus for loving service to others, in the common struggle with neighbor for justice and the assertion of humanity in the midst of degradation. This is not to be sentimental.

The power of mission in the world and the relevance of mission for the work of the world is in the freedom given to those who witness to God's work in this world to confront and cope with the world as it is: without romanticism, without indifference to any actual experience of men at work, without rationalization, without imagining that the world is different from what it is, without evasion, without escape from the real burden of daily work, which is the burden of death. A mark of work as mission is unabashed realism about the world and the work of the world.[1]

This is easy to affirm, but illustrations of such confident mission in the world are hard to come by in American church life. Much of the work of the growing lay centers is focused at the point of witness in daily work, through or in spite of the nature of the task itself. The Christian Faith and Life Community in Austin, seeking to penetrate the college community, and the Detroit Industrial Mission, directly engaged with heavy industry in Detroit, may produce much of help to the whole church in the years ahead, as indeed they have already done.

In this country we need to recognize that men and women who hold jobs are almost certainly involved in vocational communities. Persons on the same street and in the same apartment building rarely know one another, but within the city the doctors know one another, and so do the truck drivers. There are real communities of existence. It is into these that the church must penetrate, even if specialized ministries are needed. Theological reflection and the appropriate sacramental life of the Christian community need to take place in the context where decisions must be made and in which obedience is required. Such expressions of congregational

[1] "Work as Mission," a Study Outline. World's Student Christian Federation, Geneva, 1960.

147

life, as they take shape in a variety of situations, may well become normative in the years ahead.

The World of Home

Here the significance for the congregation has already been implied in the illustration of the door seals. In a missionary congregation the homes in which God's people dwell are open to the world and are in themselves an expression of the reconciliation to which they point.

In the particular situation where these door seals were used, not only did they serve to symbolize the dispersion of the church into the world, but the message of the door seal had a rather surprising effect on some of the church members. Now their home was no longer their castle, a place of refuge against the world, but it was supposed to bear the marks of the church itself. If the church was expected to be open to all people, the door seal implied that so their home was expected to be open. Now a man's home was no longer a refuge from the world, but a base of operations from which to move into the world. If a Bible study group met in his apartment, then he had to welcome everyone in the name of Christ—including his enemies, the disagreeable woman downstairs, or the drunk who stumbled into the meeting. Sometimes when men make simple symbolic gestures what they have done or said requires them to be better than they want to be. It is quite possible, I think, to suggest that this may be one of the ways in which God's grace is at work, seeking to remind men that the place where they live is not their own but God's. In their homes they are to be a living witness to Christ.

The experience of the urban priests with their open rectory may serve as a parable against which every Christian needs to determine the relation of his own home and family to the world. C. Kilmer Myers wrote:

We did not exactly plan our life in the rectory. People in the parish and from the neighborhood just began coming in; we did not stop them.

Soon we began to realize that coming over to the "parish," as they say, filled a tragic need, at least in part. They wanted a "community"; they wanted to be with other people; not with other people in the Hudson Tube or in a cheap movie emporium, but in a decent house. Most of them did not have decent houses. . . . The rectory *had* to be open.[2]

There is an obvious tension between the need for withdrawal and return, for a place of rest and comfort away from the struggles in the world. At the same time, however, the witness of the homes of a congregation involves them precisely in this tension, whose resolution is never satisfactory. To avoid the conflict is to deny God. To accept it may be to find that he grants the strength and wisdom and, above all, the gift of love to bear it with joy. To the degree that Christian homes reflect the same reality as the gathered life of the congregation, to that degree there is integrity. The home is part of the sacramental community. Its Christian service is the whole theme of salvation.

The Neighborhood

The problem of city life involves among other things the matter of leisure time. The church's answer too often is to draft people into spending as much time as possible in the manifold activities and enterprises within the church building. For the missionary congregation the task is the reverse: To capture a large share of people's leisure time, but to expend it in the world. A new understanding of "parish," even in churches with a quite different tradition, has been a strong asset in making explicit the responsibility of a congregation for its neighborhood. The church as a gathered congregation of believers is deeply concerned to affirm that the whole community is its parish and that no one living in the immediate area is beyond its concern. The neighborhood, for Christians, must cease to be part of the private sphere and become part of the public arena, with the focus upon

[2] C. Kilmer Myers, "Second Address," General Theological Seminary (April, 1950), p. 24.

community action that will release and direct the vitalities of human life.

The neighborhood, as the immediate concern of the congregation, is an important locus of obedience and service. In this context Christ is at work. He will be found where he said he would meet us, in the form of strangers and prisoners and neighbors. Where there is human need, where the processes of dehumanization warp and twist human life—there Christ is to be found, calling men back to their true humanity. There the congregations must be in dispersion. A symbol is important. Several city parishes now require as part of their covenant of membership that those entering the congregation join at least one community group that is working for brotherhood or justice. This is a sign of their commitment to enter into Christ's work in the world, for through such organizations God's will is being accomplished.

In these involvements in community life the Christian seeks ways to bring to bear his concern for reconciliation. Prerequisite for reconciliation is continual attention to making all human relationships personal. The strength of Christians lies in the person-to-person encounter. The master strategy must be to direct all our activities to bringing this about. Without the encounter no strategy is complete, but without a strategy no encounter is probable.

To enter into the ministry of Christ in the world is to be engaged, then, at all the normal places where life's business takes one. This is to take the worldliness of Bonhoeffer seriously, to live as a free human being with nothing better to do than share the burden of Christ through the love of neighbor. Love is thus the test of the Christian's obedience in relation to his neighbor. In relation to the structures of society love must find expression in justice. This is primarily a corporate issue, however, and will be considered in the following chapter.

One important footnote is required about the meaning of neighborhood for suburban congregations. Is it fair to suggest that for them neighborhood must be no less than metropolis? Only as those who earn their living in the central city, but reside in the suburbs, come to feel an abiding responsibility for metropolis as their "neighborhood" and give serious attention to its problems and needs is there any source of leadership and effective power sufficient for the needs that must be met. For the suburbanite, public responsibility is not fulfilled by working for better schools in his residential community, for this is still within the private realm. His concern must be for decent schools in the whole metropolis.

Neighborhood
Obedience Further Considered

In this section of the chapter we have been concerned with living by the way of the cross and have indicated that the Christian is called to this obedience in the various arenas in which his life is played out. Now we shall take one of these areas, the neighborhood, and indicate in somewhat greater depth the implications for the Christian in this context. These may provide some specific guidance, not only in this arena, but for the others as well. I shall suggest four guidelines for the Christian who seeks in concrete terms to participate in Christ's ministry in his neighborhood.

1. *The Christian enters into community organizations.* The suggested participation in voluntary organizations is not in order to make individuals Christian but that they may serve as salt or leaven, fermenting the organization, or giving it the flavor of a perspective that is not bound simply by the organization and its goals. For example, after many years in East Harlem, worried by their withdrawal from the area of community organization, two settlement houses embarked on "The East Harlem Project." With substantial foundation backing, they hired a core of unusually competent and sensitive social workers to provide resources for whatever community leadership might still exist in the neighborhood. The astonishing results of this project is another story, but in helping organize tenants' associations in the public-housing projects, parents' associations in the local schools, and then area-wide organizations in both these fields, the project provided for

151

the members of inner-city churches a new opportunity in thoroughly secular terms to take their ministry seriously. Here was a channel of community participation that rightly could demand the energy and time of the dispersed Christian. God was using these as vehicles for his missionary task. Through them men were struggling against the depersonalization of urban life and were seeking to give expression to their humanity. In East Harlem today one finds church members directing political clubs, leading parents' associations in the schools, working in tenants' groups, joining the civil rights struggle, and in these and other commitments expressing their obedience to Christ, not as a diversion from church work but precisely as expressions of their commitment to obedience.

There remains in congregational thinking great vagueness about the meaning of involvement in community organizations. What does a Christian add to the secular situation by his presence, or what does he contribute that is unique? Does he seek to introduce God or inculcate Christian principles? If we are on the right track in our understanding, the Christian is above all to be present as a worldly man sharing fully in the task of the organization, with no special competence from his ethical armory, but with a "secular wisdom"—an understanding of God's purpose for the world—that illuminates and defines the situation. In quite specific terms, in a secular organization the meaning of Christian involvement can be spelled out as in these suggestions from Horst Symanowski, long devoted to industrial work in the German church:

1. Keeping organizations prepared to accept changes, and on the move;
2. Standing by their officials and ensuring that they do not despise people, or manipulate them—because Jesus preferred to be despised himself rather than to despise someone else;
3. Breaking down all taboos, and tackling awkward questions; revealing that it is a sin to cling to the status quo or to justify doing so on religious grounds, because by clinging to what is old we prevent ourselves from making a new beginning and creating a new situation;
4. Refusing to accept hostilities between people as final;

5. Breaking down barriers between races, nations, religions and ideologies, and building bridges of understanding.

2. *The Christian will enter into politics.* The obvious vehicle in most situations for community participation is party politics. A good deal of false idealism has been written in this field, suggesting, for example, that Christians ought all at once to join a local party. The fact that they are highly suspect and often unwanted is such a shock that many simply withdraw for good. Politics is important, but it must be entered into with comprehension and humility. This is the path of "relevant love." It is God's vehicle for ordering human life in community. Many of the crucial problems of the city can be faced and political pressure exerted by quasi-political pressure groups like those organized by the East Harlem Project. Ultimately, however, citizen participation in the direct party machinery is essential for the health of both the city and the democratic society. Again, here we are not concerned with a treatise on the Christian in politics, but with affirming that in a missionary congregation this is where the battle lies.

The church will have failed miserably in its response and obedience to God if we do not send into the political work selfless and dedicated persons girded with the faith that this is where God intends them to be—obedient in the life and death struggle for survival and freedom. The political process is also the object of God's redeeming love and power.[3]

Several years ago in East Harlem a heterogeneous group of citizens, prodded and assisted by members of the Reformed Democratic Movement in New York City, began to meet to discuss how the great majority of East Harlem residents, apathetic and disinclined to political participation, might accept their responsibility as citizens. In the nucleus that brought into being an East Harlem Reformed Democratic Club were a number of members of the East

[3] Howard Moody, "The Church Must Face Hard Political Realities," *The Intercollegian* (April, 1960).

Harlem Protestant Parish who felt that they were simply fulfilling their responsibility as Christians in a democratic society through their political involvement. In remarkably short order, in part through a campaign that registered 3,400 new voters, the Reformed Club gained control of the party machinery from the small clique that had ruled their particular assembly district for generations. The East Harlem Protestant Parish, accustomed to struggle against the political machinery of East Harlem, suddenly discovered that both district leaders were committed members of its churches and able to articulate the meaning of their faith for their political involvement.

Once involved, the battered Christian will turn with new need to the gathered life of the church for insight, healing, and direction. In that context, a study group on the Christian in politics can suddenly come alive. Perhaps now the "secular" wisdom of the gospel will begin to make sense, and men will discover that the gospel comprehends the reality of a world of compromise, of power and decision, and gives to the man of faith the understanding and conviction to live and work within it. This is no absolute ethical position to be imposed on each situation, but a confidence in the grace of God by which men may dare to take the risk of action and, even when they fail, may hope for forgiveness and be sustained anew.

3. *The center of concern is real need.* Part of the wisdom of faith is discerning both immediate need and ultimate need in one's brother. Peter, asked for alms by the beggar at the gate, gave healing instead. Jesus fed the hungry with food, but he reminded them of their deeper hunger that bread alone could not fill. Thus compassion for those in need is supplemented with the kind of comprehension that is concerned with more than the immediate problem. A drug addict needs food and encouragement to accept medical care. Ultimately, he needs a community of love and acceptance. At the same time, something must be done about the narcotics traffic that takes men into bondage.

The answer to men's needs, with all the necessary effort to

meet the immediate problems, is to become human again and to be maintained in their humanity. For this Christ, not all the human schemes put together, is finally sufficient. To Christ, and not to their program to help drug addicts, men must point. It is his healing and love they mediate. This obvious fact is betrayed in reality by individual Christians again and again. In their humanness, needing to be appreciated, they expect thanks and gratitude. But a missionary congregation serves for Christ's sake alone. To him is the honor and the praise.

The tension for individuals and for a congregation finds expression at many points. One is the sheer pressure of human need wherever they look. Where to begin and whom to help? Christian service is not promiscuous. It must decide what is its business and what must be left alone. This is perhaps the hardest decision of all in the inner city. The individual clergyman is lost from the start if he is not surrounded by a community which helps bear the load. Even so, what is a possible principle of discrimination among those who stand in need? We shall suggest more fully in a later section that this principle is found in the responsibility of the Christian for those who have no other source of help, for the unclaimed victims of injustice and oppression.

Another form of the tension is between the immediate pressures of need and the long term struggle for justice. This point is of such importance that I offer one illustration from a tragic mission situation, Sicily, where a dedicated group of Protestants have recently begun their ministry. Tullio Vinay, writing of the conflict between the urgency of the moment and the larger battle, suggested:

This is what happens. Today we take Turiddu into our home and offer to teach him how to read and write, but in less than ten days five children are coming along to be taught. . . . So that immediately our time has been divided into a thousand small activities; and it is not to do these things that we have come here, but to solve certain fundamental problems. . . .

This is our problem: should we ignore individual needs and, in order to help everyone, aim to reach the goals we have before us speedily, without wasting time and energy in giving individual help or in charitable action? Or should we simply, first and foremost, take notice of those we meet, young and old, and be near them to help them, thinking of them as those whom the Lord sends to us?

I think our position with regard to this problem must be dialectical: it will give no peace to our hearts, but perhaps for this very reason is more alive and true than any established doctrine of well planned charity or thoroughly organized social reform. We should never lose sight of the general problem and face it with firmness and farsightedness, but we should not ever shut our eyes and our hearts before those we meet on our way. We should not allow ourselves to be caught up entirely by small everyday happenings, but we should not even make an alibi for ourselves of a programme that is worthy of the name. . . . All this is far from easy; it leaves us dissatisfied, yet there is no way out of it. Christ preached the Kingdom, that is the reason why He came, yet from morning to night people who needed him crowded around him.[4]

4. *Loving service is its own justification.* The relation between service and the increase of church membership has often been seen by the congregation as a direct one. We argue that in a missionary congregation service which grows out of a personal relationship of love, the "unlimited liability" of the one for the other, to use the fine Quaker phrase, finds sufficient justification for action in the need of the other person. There is no ulterior motive, for the Lord of the church is not served by gaining "rice Christians." Even though the ultimate need of every person is for life in a community centered in Christ, the acts of service are not a kind of bait. The Christian must ask why he is doing an act of service, for as much self-understanding as possible provides some defense, not only against false evangelism, but also against his own unconscious motivations in "helping others."

If the deeds are signs of Christ, then he will use them as he sees fit. When the congregation in its service in dispersion grows concerned about response to its service it ventures onto dangerous ground. This is a difficult matter to state adequately, for if men

[4] "Man and His Programmes," *Riesi,* a News Letter (March, 1962).

have found life in Christ they wish desperately to share their knowledge. This is right, but any method that seduces or coerces the hearer, no matter how subtle, is not of Christ. The response of Christian love does not have any ulterior motive or evangelistic purpose. Bonhoeffer wrote, "Christ died for the world, not for the church!" So Christians in dispersion, as evangelists, are called solely to share in the activity of God, not to an endeavor, however subtle or covert, to augment the churches.

5. *The Christian is in the way of the cross.* In concluding this section on the mission of the dispersed congregation it is well to remember that it was headed in subtitle, "The Reality of the Crucifixion." The setting of Christian service is suffering, amid the brokenness of life and the frustrations of depersonalization.

White clergy in the inner city, desiring with sincerity and in faith to serve Christ, find themselves often subjected to a grim testing. They claim they are brothers to Negroes who spend their lives taking orders from white men. Their claim, perhaps unconsciously, is not accepted at least until it has been subjected to ruthless testing. This is only a parable of the kind of testing to which every Christian in dispersion is put by a world that sometimes does not dare to take love seriously, sometimes in its own misery refuses it, or sometimes even kills it. How hard it is to internalize this confession so that the congregation accepts the way of a cross.

That the preaching of the Gospel and the demonstration of its power call forth a corresponding manifestation of the opposing force of evil should neither surprise nor dismay the Church. God's sovereignty is unshaken; He uses even His enemies to set forward His purposes of judgment and mercy. The Church's task remains that of faithful witness, and the Christians can with a good courage join issue with their opponents. In the last resort, the Church's strength lies in suffering endured with hope, and prayer offered in persevering love.[5]

[5] "Theological Reflections on the Missionary Task of the Church," p. 8.

The
Reality of the Resurrection

In the world the missionary congregation, through its members in dispersion, enters into the ministry of its Lord. It works without ceasing in all places and at all times. In keeping pace with Christ, however, it lives by faith and not by works. The paradox of mission is that the work of Christians is not determined by any concrete achievements or victories won, but lies solely in the truth of the resurrection. The Christian points to his living Lord, to the victory that has been won, to the hope that is sure, as the substance of life now in the world. To make and keep men truly human is to point to Christ, to his activity and authority and to his ultimate victory.

When men truly encounter Christ in the power of the resurrection, they may be led to accept his lordship and themselves enter into his work in the world. This is themselves to be evangelized. An evangelizing congregation, one that is entering into the incarnation, engaged in the way of the cross, will also be pointing continually to its Lord, for in the resurrection lies its hope. It is impossible to devise any strategy for living by the resurrection. If Christ is Lord, is alive to a congregation, then they naturally point to him as the truth by which they live and work. Christians have always found ways to confess the faith that sustains them. In this section I will suggest some of the possible structures through which men may express this hope and thus become themselves witnesses to the resurrection.

1. *They will point to Christ in nonverbal ways.* Often these days writers return to the metaphor of "first fruits," reminding us that the Christian community is the sign of the harvest, pointing to the eschatological conclusion that awaits the world. This idea makes the particular place in which the Christian finds himself, however insignificant, of central importance. His presence is imperative as a sign in terms of Christian presence and involvement in the concrete place of work and ordinary life, as a symbolical representation of the new humanity in Jesus Christ. Every Chris-

tian as first fruits is placed in a concrete social context as a sign of the new humanity, as one who is able, by God's grace, to pay the price of taking upon himself the needs, anxieties, and sufferings of his fellowmen in the world. Just as the risen Christ showed his hands and his side to his disciples, so the marks of suffering are the credentials of the resurrected life. The Christian points to his Lord as he lives in his suffering in and for the world. But first fruits involve as fully the signs of reconciliation and joy that are the blessings of life as part of the new family of Christ. The Christian makes visible something of the new order of life in Christ as it effects all his relationships. He is a sign that God's gifts have in fact come to men.

2. *They will talk about Christ.* A recent inner city lectionary is built around the theme of "gossiping the gospel." A missionary congregation is concerned that all its members in their dispersion talk naturally about their Lord. To share the good news with hope of being heard in our day must involve two essentials. One is that the individual's whole life be so full of thanksgiving and love for Christ that this reality spills over naturally into his talk and actions. In this sense Christ's presence is a continual reality, making him a sort of third person in every action and conversation. Thus the phrase about gossiping the gospel. If the resurrection is a living reality for men they inevitably talk about it, not to pressure others into belief, but simply and directly, as something that is real and important.

In the second place, to talk about Jesus Christ must not only become as natural as gossip, but also must not be an intrusion which insists that others listen to the Christian on his terms. To gossip is not at all to insist that others talk to us about their religious faith or lack of it. The missionary congregation in dispersion, working in Christ's name, must be prepared to discuss its faith when people ask, but not always be insisting that it be given a hearing. When the congregation is engaged in its rightful tasks again and again the world asks questions: Why struggle with such hopeless tasks; why do you not quit; what are you getting out of it; why do you remain so confident and cheerful when people kick you in the teeth all the time? Then the Christian has the opportunity to speak about the victory of his Lord and in a new and fresh way point to the resurrection.

The Christian has to leave the work of conversion in the hands of God. His job is to sow, and when the harvest comes, to reap. But God gives the increase. A useful illustration comes from the story of Peter and the crowd in Acts 2. The crowd listened to Peter speak of the gospel only after they had seen the power of the Holy Spirit. Demonstration preceded the word of witness. In particular, note that Peter had no commercial at the end, no plea to accept Jesus or be converted. He stated his case and that was it. Only when some in the crowd asked, with urgent concern, "What must we do to be saved," did Peter fulfill his role of harvesting, leading them by repentance and baptism into the new life in Christ. The culmination was their ordination for their role in Christ's missionary work, the baptism of the Holy Spirit. Thus even in this story, so often mistakenly used to justify the mass evangelism methods of our time, the conversion was left to God. But when it happened, it was entirely within the context of the missionary explosion of the church, the real significance of Pentecost.

This point of view has specific implications for the great American tradition of evangelism which has involved two different aspects. One has been visitation, and the other has been the evangelistic revival. Neither of these seems to make sense any longer as the way in which the church can point to the activity of God. They are primarily useful for dealing with those who are already living within the shadow of the Christian faith and who have some memory to which they can be called back. They do not help us to understand what God is doing in the world, nor are they even heard by the world that stands outside any real relationship with the church. They both lend themselves unfortunately to institutionalism, to a program designed to build an institution. Increasingly they have no relevance to genuine evangelism, to the work of the church as a light on a hill pointing to the activity of God.

For instance, in a large public-housing project live many members of a nearby congregation. How tragic if the congregation must organize a program of visitation evangelism in order to call on the people in that project. God has put members of that congregation into the various buildings precisely in order that they might be witnesses to Christ. They are the ones who live there naturally and whose daily lives either gossip the gospel or deny Christ. It is a sign of weakness if some special crusade must be organized in order that the church might begin to do what its members by rights should be doing by their presence there in the midst of the community already. A special calling program by the congregation as such may at times be in order and helpful, but basically the task of witness will be dependent on the work of those who live there.

3. *They will pray.* Prayer is part of the action of witness. When all doors of spoken witness are closed, intercession remains the business of the Christian. He is able always and everywhere to pray for the work in which he is engaged, but even when all seems hopeless he still lifts his concern for his brother to God—to wait, to share, to hope, and always to pray. Prayer is thus a part of active waiting for the right time. To be a witness is to sow and to wait in humility, in humility because the seed which we sow has to die, in hope because we expect that God will quicken this seed and give it its proper body. Evangelism is never surprised by whatever results God chooses to give. We dare not focus our attention on the growth of the congregation. This is God's business. Whenever the church grows concerned at this point mission is replaced by "churchification." Men are called to enter into God's task, to speak of him when the opportunity offers itself, but they are to be content even as they pray to leave the final decision in God's hand. God will determine whether the word falls upon rocky or thorny soil, or indeed may chance upon good soil and grow. The willingness to leave this matter in God's hands is difficult, but men must harvest indeed only when God does give the increase.

4. *They will trust in the Resurrection.* After having done all, but

not before, the Christian leaves the verdict in God's hands. In the end he lives by hope, by faith in the resurrection. This is not an easy reality for Americans to take seriously. It is hard to believe that men cannot learn how to communicate the gospel so that effectiveness and "success" are guaranteed. Their witness is not based on personal experience, however, but on a mighty act of God that to the world continues to be shocking and unacceptable. Dr. Hoekendijk wrote:

This point should be emphasized for it is precisely in evangelistic work that we run the risk of minimizing this feature of revelation. The temptation to mask the mystery, to avoid the scandal of the Gospel, becomes almost inevitable, once we are confronted with men who are perplexed by the absurdity of our message.

In this predicament men tend to fall back on pious generalities or personal witness that is not refutable.

The Christian lives in dispersion by hope. Entering into the life of the work, taking up the work of Christ, he continues by the reality of the resurrection which is God's assurance that the victory over evil in the world is secure. This is to live in what Paul Tillich describes as the "boundary-situation." The Christian's existence is symbolized on the one hand by a vertical relationship which reminds him of his absolute dependence upon God's grace and reminds him that he is never fully in the world, but lives always by what Tillich calls "the religious reservation." At the same time, his life is symbolized by a horizontal line that reminds him of his religious obligation, his responsibility to be involved in the world as Christ was in the world. "Hope unites the vertical and the horizontal lines, the religious reservation and the religious obligation. Therefore, the ultimate word that religion must say to the people of our time is the word of hope." [6] This is not to put off to a distant or hidden future the obedience and vision which seem too hard for the present, but to make it possible for men here and

---

[6] Tillich, *The Protestant Era* (Chicago: University of Chicago Press, 1948), p. 191.

now to work in the power and by the light of that which is still to come.

Issues
for Missionary Structures

This chapter has sought to define and describe patterns of lay involvement in the mission of Christ to the world. The goal is Christians, self-consciously engaged in service and witness wherever they find themselves, seeking not to impose predetermined solutions on the problems they find, but in the process of genuine confrontation and participation, to live as true human beings. "In our time we may be unable to see the way out of the human problems of the world. But the way in is clearly evident. It is to invest our lives in the service of those problems as they bear upon people." [7] In bringing this chapter to a conclusion, there are four areas requiring attention.

Congregational Organization

Again we discover that the clear demand of mission is that the multiplicity of congregational organizations be eliminated. A missionary congregation does not need a women's missionary society, but women engaged in mission. For male fellowship let the men join the Rotary or the union and in that context become salt that preserves the secular structures of community. The ecclesiastical chaos which this proposal seems to invite is actually highly unlikely. In the rare congregations that have in fact given up these special church organizations, such as Church of the Saviour in Washington, D.C., the involvement of the congregation in mission has been reflected also in a very large amount of missionary giving. In the study groups of the congregation the wisdom and experience of overseas missions may have a relevance and influence that is far more significant than the usual effect of a mission speaker describing native life in some

[7] Kenneth Cragg, *The Call of the Minaret* (New York: Oxford University Press, 1956), p. 214.

163

far-off land. The small groups in a congregation, along with the vestry, session, or governing board, can manage to fulfill the necessary institutional requirements of the congregation without setting up a host of organizations to fill out in full a denominational table of organization for the local church. One illustration serves as an indication of this line of argument. Many churches now raise their budget by an every-member canvass that requires considerable planning and organization. In several inner-city parishes where the Bible study groups spread across the parish, each assumes responsibility for canvassing their area, since they will be calling for Bible study in any case. It sounds simple and is simple.

Thus we conclude that congregational organization must be functional for mission. The time in small groups must have one eye always on the worldly involvements of their members, so that the precious time the church requires will be used for equipping the saints. It is still the rare pastor who affirms to his congregation, "I would far rather have any one of you get into the political struggle in this city than belong to a hundred committees in the parish." [8]

To abandon clericalized, religious activity for a serious development of the lay apostolate, to surrender the sentimentality of pietistic Christianity for the harsh realities of public responsibility, these are difficult transformations to contemplate with equanimity; nevertheless, they are the changes called for by the new frontier of American domestic life—the task of shaping the metropolis as a human community.[9]

Doctrine of the Laity Reconsidered

Can the laity enter into the world along the lines suggested in this chapter? There is not much evidence from the inner city to go on, but here and there positive signs have emerged. In New York the members of the East Harlem Protestant Parish have entered in a surprising degree into the task of service in

[8] C. Kilmer Myers, quoted in the *Herald Tribune*, September 24, 1962, p. 21.
[9] Gibson Winter, address, "The New Christendom in the Metropolis" (June, 1962), page 6.

their community, participating in a variety of secular organizations and political parties. The key has been not only in the theology of the parish and the faith of the members, but also in the presence of sensitive social workers who have faith in the people and who believe that given support, not direction, from professionals the community will bring forth unexpected leadership and determination. This has indeed happened, as the experience in East Harlem testifies.

We would conclude that in spite of the human problems of inner city life, with all their deadening effects, there is leadership potential that can be aroused where people are taken seriously. The congregation in dispersion can be a powerful leaven in this fermenting process.

At one point some confusion does arise. In the theological consensus it was noted that the clergyman was called to work within the gathered life of the church, equipping the laity for their mission in the world. The world responds to the professional status of the clergyman, however. It is the clergyman who can get through to the welfare supervisor and push aside the delays for a family in need. The judge listens to the clergyman standing beside a boy in trouble. In some of these situations, even if it means a compromise with his theology, the clergyman in the inner city must accept the professional status in the world that opens vital secular doors. But he does well to remember that such involvement is not a function of ordination and can in fact be developed and encouraged in non-ordained members who have the time for such professional work or through the staff employment of social caseworkers. In other words, even as all the laity seek to take seriously the priesthood of all believers, there remain professional aspects of referral that demand special competence.

The Reality of Dispersion

Does the description here of the laity in dispersion take adequately into account the realities of the world of the inner city? In terms of the problems of human life, it would seem that many facts are confronted head on. If the problem is leisure time, here is a way of life that promises to give meaning in place of boredom, significant use of time instead of time to be killed. For the Christian there is always work to do and urgent demands on his time. If the problem is lack of meaning in work, this perspective seeks to transcend the frustrations of monotony by focusing on obedience in every situation. Such an attitude to the world tries in every way to take the facts of man's existence seriously, to listen honestly, and yet to continue to struggle against dehumanization with hope. In a word, we argue that a missionary congregation is utterly realistic about the world and yet lives with the kind of confidence that brings hope in apathy, love in anomie, and direction in meaninglessness.

A Footnote on the Clergy

The emphasis of this chapter on the central role of the laity as the church at work in the world has important implications for the role of the clergy. It demands no less than that the clergy live fully in the world as men; on the frontier between God and every human being; subjected to the same temptations, frustrations, and doubts; entering into the same struggle for faith as every man. In a word, the minister must dare to be honest about who he is—a forgiven sinner standing in daily need of God's grace. Only in this way may he hope that all the human barriers of race, class, and education, as well as the wall of ordination, may be overcome.

This is hard for the minister to internalize. A number of recent surveys have indicated how many in the ministry have been called to this vocation in part out of a deep need to please people. It is certainly true that the minister is looked upon as a person who is supposed to please everybody, to be well thought of both by the members of the church and by the world. This is a difficult position, likely to blunt the prophetic voice and to lead to tremendous internal conflicts and frustrations as a minister seeks to be a servant of God and a servant of men. The clergy must learn to speak the truth in love, to bear the pain and conflict and tension which may result in the life of the church, and to serve God first and the church second. There is no ultimate conflict between the two, but men create one when they seek to be the cheerful parson, loved and respected by all.

The clergyman must also live in the world as well as in the church. He is a citizen, probably a husband and father, and has other roles as well. While there is no consensus on this point at all, I suggest that in these worldly relationships the clergyman ought to function as a layman, for nothing in his ordination prepares him for any privileged role in the world. His ordained functions are in the church. In the world he is part of the body of Christ along with all other laity. These worldly roles demand his participation responsibly as a sign to the congregation if nothing else. Above all, if he is to take seriously the incarnation, he and his family must live in the parish and share fully in its life. City clergy who commute to their parishes make a sad witness.

Sharp issues for the clergy emerge at two further points. First is the present misunderstanding of the pastoral role of the minister. To be a faithful pastor is not to accept as the focus of one's work the role of personal counselor, helping people face their personal crises. To bear one another's burdens is a legitimate function for the whole congregation, as well as a specialized role for professional counselors. Even if the minister tried, he could not possibly meet such needs in his parish, whether we think in terms of an inner city parish of several hundred or a suburban church of one thousand. The basic pastoral role of the clergyman is in a somewhat different focus: to discover, release, and direct the gifts of ministry that Christ has surely bestowed on members of his congregation. If the priesthood of all believers is to take on reality, those with genuine gifts of ministry must be enabled to use them for the sake of the whole body and in their obedience in the world. Of course, as part of his own life in Christ the clergyman is also a burden bearer, but he must not take into his own hands the primary ministry and thus frustrate the authentic ministries of the whole body. The fact

167

is that most clergy insist on the central counseling role, to the effective exclusion of their authentic pastoral task and most church members expect and demand it. This expectation a missionary congregation must challenge.

The clergy are even more threatened by the new stance of congregational life that makes the important work of the Christians in the world rather than in the institutional life of the church. Traditionally the clergyman has become like the chief executive of a large corporation. He is the center around which the life of the congregation rotates. How difficult for the clergy to release their laity for work in the world! How much more difficult to relinquish the idea that the clergy are to have ultimate oversight and control of the life of the congregation! There is little room for the work of the Spirit if the minister must always be consulted before significant decisions are made. Rather, a missionary congregation will develop an image of the clergyman not as the chief executive of a flourishing organization, but as a chaplain to the laity in their mission to the world, as one who assists the laity in the work of God in making and keeping men truly human. In this light, the role of the clergy will assume its proper place within the gathered life of the church, not as superior or more important, but simply as a vital and necessary part of the total missionary purpose of the congregation.

Finally, the clergy need to be part of a disciplined group that sustains them. In every neighborhood clergy are called to find men, perhaps of other denominations, who also recognize the need for a sustaining functional group. If such is necessary for the Christian style of life, then it must be found at all costs. Here and there city pastors are uniting in group ministries that cut across denominational lines and become an effective part of the lives of those involved.[10]

---

[10] For information about one inner-city pattern, write to East Harlem Protestant Parish, 2050 Second Avenue, New York, N.Y.

8
THE
CONGREGATION
IN MISSION

"God is at work in the world." This
basic theological affirmation must be expressed by the corporate
life of the congregation and not left simply to the individual laity
in dispersion. The church exists as an institution in a world of
institutions and does not dare avoid accepting its destiny as a missionary instrument in God's hands. When the churches of our day
leave the work of mission entirely to individual laity and reject
any significant corporate confrontation between the institution and
the world, they do not thus escape from involvement with the
world. They simply become supporters of the status quo. In our

day, in a world of massive structures and pyramids of power, the congregation as a whole must enter into the work of God. Even now his kingdom is breaking in upon the world, restoring men to their true humanity. The church, in sharing in God's politics, is called to discern what God is doing, to share in his task, and finally to point to what God is doing.

We shall examine the material of this chapter under these three headings. This is not at all an absolute division into three parts which must be followed in some kind of sequence, but rather an effort to find categories by which we may begin to understand the dimensions of the task of God's people. Note also that the headings used for the three sections of this chapter parallel and develop the headings of the previous chapter (Incarnation, Crucifixion, Resurrection). In the preceding chapter we have discussed the structures that may enable the members in dispersion to enter into the work of obedience in the world. Here we are concerned with the structures that enable a congregation as a whole to join in the task of God's politics; that is, making and keeping men truly human. In each concrete situation the relation between the congregation as a whole and the individual witness of its members is almost surely intertwined. Thus the division here into separate chapters is a little artificial, but some such scheme is necessary for the sake of clarity. Also time and again we need reminders that individual action on the old assumption that "converted individuals will convert the world" is no longer tenable, but a disastrous misunderstanding of the mission of the congregation.

One word of caution is in order. In considering the missionary structure for the congregation, Christians need to remember that the church is called to be an instrument of God, not a third party in its own right which stands over against the world. The two great realities of which we speak are God and the world. God is at work in the church and in the world. The church is simply called to join God in his work. The world is the locus of its mission. A congregation is truly the church only insofar as it discerns this continuing mission of God to the world and shares in it.

Such a theological affirmation provokes a strenuous judgment upon present church life. Rather than serving in and for the world, the churches have divorced themselves in large part from society. The current dispute over the proper relations between the church and the state points to the problem most clearly. In Colonial days the churches had a clearly understood function, a prophetic and responsible one, in society. Separation of church and state made the fulfillment of this role possible. With the progressive secularization of religion and culture and the fusing of Protestantism into what Will Herberg calls "the common faith of American society," the church has lost its role and become a religious compartment (one of twenty-two departments in *Time* magazine). Today most Protestants assume that the slogan of separation of church and state means *absolute* separation. This has rendered the churches innocuous or irrelevant in American life. It may be that in the racial crisis of our time a gracious God is literally forcing the churches to corporate public responsibility and thus seeking to recall them to their authentic mission. Nowhere is the power of darkness so apparent as in racial discrimination. Unless congregations can enter here into God's work of restoring men to true humanity, they are utterly and completely irrelevant to the struggles of our time. The fact that most congregations are confused and baffled as to how to respond and act makes all the more urgent the search for structures that will enable them to engage in their mission.

To See What God Is Doing

The first task of the congregation is to discover in specific terms where God is at work in its community. This involves corporately something of the experience of individual laity in genuine participation in the world. The congregation, placed as it is in a particular setting, must listen, converse, and learn to love the world around its doors. Just as the layman in dispersion earns the right to speak of his faith when he stands alongside other men and shares their life in the world, so the congregation must enter into the world with compassion and humility, as ready to listen as to speak, if it is to be heard at all. The congregation must become an *ecclesia audiens,* a listening, sensitive body, seeking to find where God is at work in the needs of men rather than to impose its judgments upon the world.

Sometimes the world even pleads for such understanding and empathy. A personnel manager for a large organization, taking issue with some too glib statements from the church, wrote:

Yes, let the church speak, but first let it listen! Let it become deeply, seriously immersed in the concerns, problems and aspirations of all who labor, even the organization man. Let professors of business management, articulate managers of industry, competent labor leaders be heard in seminaries and minister groups.

Let churchmen read broadly in the professionally written material for business managers, which seeks to help them come to grips with the problems of business operation in our changing environment. Let ministerial candidates serve as interns in business—not as chaplains but as actual participants in the business enterprize. Gradually, then, the church will gain more creditability in its pronouncements on the economic order—the trumpet will sound a more certain note! [1]

For many Protestant congregations such a listening presence in the world will have to take on a hard and difficult challenge. The community with which the congregation in suburbia will have to be concerned is not simply its own neighborhood, but also—and perhaps primarily—the entire metropolitan area of which it is a part. God is at work, seeking to redeem cities and make them again the locus of full human life. As was suggested earlier, only as those who draw their economic strength from the city but escape at night to suburbia feel bound to the struggle of the whole metropolitan area are there resources in political and economic terms to make real progress. The inner-city parishes of Protestantism are in effect eyes

[1] William C. Hart, "Church and Organization Man," *The Christian Century* (October 25, 1961), pp. 1275-76.

and ears through which to recall metropolitan Protestantism to its crucial responsibility to serve in the public realm and to share in the task of rebuilding cities for human life.

In terms of missionary structures, only a few attempts have been made by individual congregations to face their role in mission. More often the task is left to denominational structures or missionary boards. In terms of a listening, serving presence in the world, the congregation of the Church of the Saviour in Washington, D. C., has taken a concrete step through its "Potter's House." This is the church seeking to break out of its building and live in the world, to listen, to confront, to witness. The experience of the past two years makes an exciting story. In describing their venture the members wrote:

The Potter's House is not a coffee house in any usual sense. It is a thrust of a church into the world—one of the ways in which we who have been called to be fishers of men are casting our nets. We are letting the world know that the church is not an institution removed from life, but a people seeking to serve those who long for a new dimension—those who for one reason or another have "written off" the church. Here we provide a setting in which the "irreligious" can ask aloud their questions. . . .

The unit of evangelism is our common life together. What we seek to do is to embody the Gospel—to be the forgiven community, the community which knows how to accept, knows how to love. It is an awesome thing to think about because we know how poorly we do it unless the Holy Spirit will work in and through us.

In the East Harlem Protestant Parish a large ministry to drug addicts grew out of the plea of several laymen that "our church has to do something about addicts." In a real sense this was the congregation looking and listening to find where God was at work and then joining in the task of service.

In large part the laity are the eyes and ears of the church, reporting back to the whole body where God is at work and what he is about. One parish now each year spends time considering the crucial areas of need that have come to light in its neighborhood and after a planning conference agrees on three or four areas in which it will concentrate its concern for the following year. This means that the laity will be consciously deployed in community organization in order to work on the defined areas. The first and basic preparation for any such decisions about deployment is to get the facts about the local community. Most denominations have developed adequate methods for undertaking such a community self-study. Some such structure of community presence and involvement would seem essential for a missionary congregation, with subsequent implementation equally necessary.

Joining in God's Task

At this point the task of the congregation will differ substantially from that of the laity in dispersion. As citizens in society laity are called to enter into the common tasks of community life. For a congregation engaged in mission there are definite criteria which need to be applied in determining what forms the action of the church as a body takes in the world. Again, we are not trying to write a book on ethics, but to offer suggestions which are directly relevant to the urban situation and which grow out of our theological consensus. Christian life in its biblical meaning is always aware of being part of God's action toward the world. "Its mission is not additional to its being. It is, as it is sent and active in its mission. It builds up itself for the sake of its mission and in relation to it." [2]

The Ministry to Human Need

To a missionary congregation there is a clear imperative to seek to mediate Christ's healing ministry to all who live in its neighborhood. Jesus gave the directive when he read from the scroll at Nazareth:

[2] Karl Barth, *Church Dogmatics*, translated by G. W. Bromiley (Edinburgh: T. & T. Clark, 1956), vol. IV, part 1, p. 725.

174

Preach good news to the poor.
He has sent me to proclaim release to the captives
and recovering of sight to the blind,
to set at liberty those who are oppressed,
to proclaim the acceptable year of the Lord. (Luke 4:18-19.)

Thus did he restore men to their true humanity. For the congregation to share in this ministry is to erect signs of the reconciliation which has come in Christ and to witness to the kingdom that is already breaking in upon men.

Even the most strenuous critics of the church are usually willing to concede the validity of the church's efforts to meet human need at the immediate personal level. In the inner city again and again it is the congregation that is sensitive and concerned about individual human problems. In New York it was discovered that all the agencies in the city offering help to drug addicts were church related, although often operating without specific religious labels. In meeting the depersonalization of modern urban life the church does seem to be relevant at many points of individual need.

The dilemma of decision remains, however. Given a situation of manifold human needs, with all the human limitations of time and energy and personnel, to whom is the ministry of the congregation offered? Promiscuous service is self-defeating and relatively useless. I would suggest that the congregation as such should enter primarily into tasks of service and obedience that give some opportunity of witnessing to the Lord who directs them there.

It cannot be the primary task of the Church to contribute to the general work of supporting, developing and improving human life. This is good and necessary work to which Christians and non-Christians alike are called. . . . But when the Church decides to render work of service to those outside, it always has to be, however broken and partial, a sign of the Kingdom, an echo and analogy of God's saving and restoring work. . . . The unique task is to be *help of the helpless.* . . . When others do it as well or even better, her service has lost its significance as a symbol of God's restoration. . . . The first task of the Church is to keep her eyes

175

open and to pray God that she may see the really helpless; and to have the courage, not only to take up the new tasks but also (which is perhaps more difficult) to give up forms of help which have lost their witness-character.[3]

The Narcotics Program of the East Harlem Protestant Parish is a good example. Here were the forgotten men and women of society who are treated as criminals and denied any real opportunity of redemption, either through medical or social-work facilities. They stood completely outside the life of any church, caught in a terrifying form of human bondage. In entering into the ministry to the drug addict this local parish not only sought to offer Christ's love to the addict, but also became a channel through which the conscience of the whole community could be awakened. By seeking out the forgotten people of society and ministering to them the church thus calls them to the attention of the whole community. Gradually in the particular problem of narcotics here mentioned the forces of social work, medicine, and other allied professions bring their resources to bear on the problem of drug addiction. Then the addict is no longer a forgotten person but is being given, at least on a minimal level, the attention that is needed for such a problem. At this point the church has fulfilled its unique function of calling attention to the hidden or forgotten point of human need and has in a very real sense witnessed to the lordship of Christ.

This raises for the church the matter of its heavy subsidy of such institutions as Christian colleges and hospitals in a day when they no longer fulfill the function of ministry to forgotten needs of men. Perhaps the time has come here in America (it has already been forced upon most younger churches) to relinquish these institutions and to recognize that it is the job of the missionary congregations of America to provide laymen who will infiltrate as Christians the boards and staffs of institutions now properly in secular hands.

[3] H. Berkhof, "The Church's Calling to Witness and to Serve," *Ecumenical Review*, X:1 (October, 1957), pp. 29-31.

The local congregation faces this issue in the use of its own facilities. They may well possess a large and imposing building with many institutional features, gym, game rooms, and the like. If the congregation belongs in the world as much as possible such a building may be a great liability. Its continuing justification must lie neither in its importance for the leisure time of the congregation nor, as in most institutional programs, in its use as an evangelistic weapon in the community. The building, since it is there, ought to be used to the limit to provide a place for the community to meet, to play, to learn, with no strings attached. The church, even in its architecture, is thus turned back into the world, opened out to it, for the sake of the world. One remembers hearing how the Brotherhood of Sleeping Car Porters, in the difficult days of anti-union feeling, found a place to meet only in churches. In the rebuilding of our cities planners have largely disregarded the need of people to meet, to meet for all the diversity of human needs and all the vitalities of life. The prudential mind asks about the cost of keeping up the building. This may not be a problem at all if the building really finds a place in the use patterns of the community.

In the inner city the church possesses great freedom to enter into the struggle for justice. In a campaign for better housing it stands with its people in common cause, not against them. There is a kind of unambiguous virtue involved when the victims of injustice in a democratic society struggle in their own self-interest. When Negroes work for equality in their own interest they are also serving the ends of democracy. The suburban Christian, concerned to end restrictive covenants in housing or to sell a home to a Negro, faces far different circumstances with his neighbors.

There are times when service must be rendered silently, without pointing to the Lord of the church. As we have suggested, full *diakonia* demands that the church explain what it is doing and point to its Lord. A congregation that loves its Lord suffers if it has to be silent. It might be asked whether, for example, the social casework in the East Harlem Protestant Parish does not present such a moment. Each day, large numbers of men and women come to the

177

Parish office to see Ramon Diaz, a laymen who is available to help people meet the immediate personal crises that beset so many families in East Harlem. With remarkable wisdom, expert manipulation of public facilities like the Welfare Department, and obvious compassion, he provides a point of human concern for all comers. Their need is all that matters. No effort, even subtly, is made to relate them to the church. It would seem, at the moment of their need, almost brazen. But a church with silent help is something like a church without Easter. It is somewhat like the situation of Christ in the trial. He was serving the whole mankind, but silently, without demonstrating his power. If a church gives aid without being able to point to Christ and does not suffer it is on a dangerous path.

Finally, the healing ministry of the missionary congregation, involving both service to those in need and the struggle for a more just society, depends upon co-operation with others. Its work is dwarfed in the face of the needs of the inner city. With great resources, only some of the problems can be faced, some needs met. The frustration of discrimination among human problems in deciding which to take up next is an exhausting one. Such different skills are needed to face the varied problems. Some of these problems—housing, unemployment, delinquency—loom so large that a congregation cannot discover even where to begin to offer a ministry. One group of Christians seeking to engage the principalities and powers can hardly find a point of contact. The work of God demands in our time a far deeper recovery of local unity than is presently known.

To Be the Church

To enter into God's task in the world is primarily to share in the ministry of healing, of reconciliation, and of justice in order that men might become truly human. But part of the task is also simply for the congregation to be the community where these same realities are expressed and made real. This is the context in which men are enabled to remain truly human. We have said all of this before and restate it here only to underline the need for the congregation in its corporate witness in the world to demonstrate the truth of the gospel. In a suffering and sinful world the congregation may pray that in its own life it will demonstrate what is hardly possible outside the church. It will show forth man's power in Christ to transcend all human differences and divisions; to live with freedom and purpose, yet in obedience to a Lord; and to enter into the life of the world with creativity and compassion. Thus do Christians represent in the midst of a country still occupied by the enemy the lordship of their victorious but still hidden King.

The world must see that it is in their gathered life that Christians find the strength and wisdom to enter into Christ's work in the world. At the table they are fed; from the pulpit they are given directions; and in intercession their life in the world is upheld before God. In the gathered life of the congregation, men are sustained in their true humanity.

For this reason, as suggested in Chapter 7, the missionary congregation is concerned about concrete and quite specific help to individual members in their dispersed life. For the congregation as a whole it is also important that it set apart time to consider the urgent issues of its time and place, to arrive at a common mind and decide what action or word is needed. This must be a continuing built-in function of congregational life, for when a crisis erupts in the community it is often too late to make faithful decisions. What it does mean is that all questions of program, order, polity, budget, and the like must give precedence to the need to give primary attention to the work of communication and witness. On every level and at every stage, order has a single purpose: *To enable the church to deploy its forces most effectively in its assigned mission in and for the world.*

The Way of Crucifixion

As for the individual Christian, so for the congregation, the path of obedience is the way of the cross. To enter into God's politics is to live by the Crucifixion, to accept the ministry of suffering with Christ for the sake of the world. To work for justice in the world, to witness to the reality of Christ against the principalities and powers of evil at large in the world is to take on a severe battle. Thus the congregation in mission expects opposition and conflict. The world continues to find the gospel a stumbling block or foolishness (I Cor. 1:23). This will always be a harsh truth for the church to accept, but it is the way of Christ. Edmund Schlink wrote:

Have we forgotten that the very strangeness, the lack of recognition and peace, are the normal situation for the Church in the world, and that recognition by the world and peace with the world represent the anomaly? The Church finds itself in this world for ever in a frontier situation, and for that reason times of persecution are less dangerous than the peace-pact with the world which respects and guarantees the historically developed state of the Church.[4]

It helps to understand that this is the normal life for the church. It is as much the congregation's work to induce conflict as to resolve it.

Many Christians have found help in appropriating for themselves this perspective of confident suffering from Dietrich Bonhoeffer. Often quoted are these words written from prison:

Later I discovered and am still discovering up to this very moment that it is only by living completely in this world that one learns to believe. One must abandon every attempt to make something of oneself, whether it be a saint, a converted sinner, a churchman (the priestly type, so-called!), a righteous man or an unrighteous one, a sick man or a healthy one. This is what I mean by worldliness—taking life in one's stride, with all its duties and problems, its successes and failures, its experiences and helplessness. It is in such a life that we throw ourselves utterly in the arms of God and participate in his sufferings in the world and watch with Christ in Gethsemane. That is faith, that is *metanoia*, and that is what makes a man and a Christian (cf. Jeremiah 45). How can success

[4] "The Pilgrim People of God," *Ecumenical Review* (October, 1952), p. 30.

make us arrogant or failure lead us astray, when we participate in the sufferings of God by living in this world? [6]

For the missionary congregation the way of the cross also means quite simply the willingness to give up old patterns, including church-sponsored institutions, comfortable forms, beloved activities, for the sake of its function. Congregations must be willing to give up their radical individualism and institutional preoccupation. Only congregations oriented to mission and not to membership and institutional success will pay the price of co-operation that does not necessarily build up the numbers of the local church, but does witness in a community to the gospel. Churches, more rigorously than individuals, hate to give up their own life for the sake of the world.

Congregations must discover their need of one another for the integrity of their own life. Just as each Christian needs the support of brothers for his life in Christ, so each congregation needs, not only the support and encouragement of other families of faith, but also their correction and chastening. In one inner-city situation several churches were part of a common parish. As Puerto Ricans moved into the area of one of the congregations no move was made to include them in the parish ministry until a sister congregation engaged in some heavy needling. The first congregation, predominately Negro, thereupon begged help from the second which had a substantial Puerto Rican membership. Several strong Puerto Rican laymen then moved from the second to the first church to assist in a developing ministry to new families in the community.

Unity in Mission

Obviously, the purview of mission must be the whole metropolitan area, for the church as a whole, even though the local cells are the heart of the missionary work of God. The local church is a small and perhaps inconsequential in-

---

[6] *Prisoner for God*, p. 169. Used by permission of The Macmillan Company and Student Christian Movement Press, publishers of the British edition *Letters and Papers from Prison*.

fluence in the vastness of a modern metropolitan area. Given many of the major forces in urban life which we have insisted the congregation must heed, its task seems at many points hopeless. In a number of cities a new and strenuous effort at a common metropolitan mission is now underway. For effective church planning, for relevance in urban renewal strategy, in speaking prophetically to the whole city, and for many other aspects of mission, this larger ecumenicity is essential.

But we are concerned for the local congregation and its part in this process. There are several places where the local congregation is involved.

1. New possibilities of ministry are opened up. When in one community churches co-operate in witness and service, then specialization is possible, differentiation of functions can be undertaken, and a united word of prophecy can be addressed. In East Harlem the Protestant Parish, instead of celebrating Easter Dawn by itself, joined several years ago with the other Protestant churches of the community for a service at a central community location. When five-hundred Protestants marched through East Harlem celebrating the Resurrection at the top of their lungs, this was a dynamic witness to the whole neighborhood.

Adequate staffing is also a far greater possibility on the basis of unity. Duplication of effort by small churches can be overcome. Above all, laity gain a sense of esprit and hope in being part of a committed, vital movement that is able to engage the world and find a hearing.

2. The local congregation can provide the whole church with the picture of life in the inner city. If we are correct in suggesting that the inner city describes in most vivid form the illness of urban life, then the whole city needs to listen to the voice of the churches exposed and involved in these places. Inner-city parishes do not primarily ask for help in their program, for Sunday-school teachers and club leaders, but seek to point out for all to see the crucial problems of metropolis and thus call suburban and inner-city churches alike to face what is their common concern. The sorry

plight of inner-city schools, the reality of poverty, and the crisis in civil rights are the problems of the whole society.

3. The congregation is involved in relationships with suburbia. Slums and suburbs need each other desperately for the wholeness and integrity of life in Christ. The resources and civic leadership of suburban Christians are needed by the inner city. The white, middle-class Protestants in their protected, homogeneous communities need to discover through relationships of mutual service the truth of the gospel that in Christ all men are one, overcoming all human barriers.[7]

We have little experience to go on at present. The only publicized example comes from the relation of First Church, Presbyterian, Oak Park, Illinois, to several inner-city situations in Chicago. The report comes with integrity and is worth study. The important point to be made here is the need for mutuality among congregations, different as they may be in socio-economic terms. For suburbia to help its poor brothers out of *noblesse oblige* can be demonic. There must not be a one-way street—suburbia giving money and time, and inner city receiving all and giving nothing. One example of a positive mutuality may indicate the kind of relationships we must seek out.

The Narcotics Committee of the East Harlem Protestant Parish set out to get hospital beds for drug addicts in New York City hospitals. A long campaign was getting nowhere. Finally it was determined to picket City Hall. At once Protestant churches in the metropolitan area were alerted and asked to join. When the day of picketing arrived the numbers from East Harlem were more than doubled by fellow Protestants from the city, including the pastors of several fashionable churches, several wealthy business men, and a number of suburban women. In such ways as this, and many others, inner-city congregations must relate themselves and be related to their brother churches.

4. The congregation can serve special ministries. The local con-

[7] Cf. illustrations in Webber, *God's Colony in Man's World*, pp. 65 ff. and pp. 72 ff.

gregation needs very much the services of retreat centers, lay-training institutes, the work of an industrial mission, and the other manifold forms of witness which must be undertaken on behalf of the local church on a metropolitan basis. These are all ways that both supplement and enrich the mission of the congregation. In particular, only the united church can really hope to gain a hearing at the point where crucial decisions are being made about the shape of the city for the generations ahead. The church, because of its disunity and its lack of missionary responsibility, is late in beginning to enter this vital process which determines so much of the context of human life. Leadership is coming from the Department of Urban Church of the National Council of Churches and is being matched in a few cities by competent local church planning.

5. Denominational relationships are another area involved. We have put this last, where we believe it belongs. This is no plea to merge Protestantism into one denomination nor is it even an attack on denominational relationships responsibly entered into. But the facts of urban life have not penetrated much of our denominational machinery. Not only are the institutionalizing pressures still great on many inner-city churches, though this is beginning to break down here and there, but almost without exception each denomination is determined to plan its own metropolitan strategy. This is the real tragedy. In East Harlem, Baptist, Methodist, Reformed, Presbyterian, Disciple, United Church of Christ, and Lutheran congregations can begin to work together in common mission, only to discover that they are expected to be a vigorous part of a denominational area strategy. In New York City, at least, every major denomination is presently developing or is well advanced in its own missionary program to evangelize the city. Even where solid theology has resulted in genuine mission rather than membership collecting, there is blindness to the tragedy of disunity. For the inner city churches competing denominationalism is folly.

There is much justification for denominational relationships. In terms of the meaning of tradition, in patterns of worship and nurture, and in theological understanding, confessional loyalties are important. In a metropolitan area there are functions that have to do with strengthening the gathered life of the congregation that are the responsibility of denominations. Summer conferences for youth, curriculum planning, the in-service training of clergy, are among the legitimate functions for a presbytery, diocese, association, or district, but mission demands that the tight hold of denominationalism be loosened.

Pointing to God's Activity

The congregation as part of its role in the politics of God must continually seek ways to point to what God has done, is doing, and will do in and for the world. Seeing history in the light of the victory of the Resurrection, the congregation speaks the truth that illuminates reality for men in the world. Confident in the ultimate victory, the congregation lives in the midst of the world by hope and in this act points to the Lord who is yet to come. In the words of Hans Ruedi-Weber, "this is the ministry of heralding the Lord's victory and His coming triumphant entry into His reign, the world."

The Prophetic
Task of the Congregation

In but not of the world, the missionary congregation seeks to share its understanding of the world with all men. This is the prophetic word which the church addresses to the world. This goes beyond church pronouncements on various ethical issues which the world may heed or ignore. The prophetic word in large part is best seen as the church endeavoring to understand what God is doing through its own internal conversation, with the world, in a sense, listening in. For example, the important "Letter to Presbyterians" by John Mackay was addressed to a denomination, setting forth the crucial issues for men in the crisis of McCarthyism. It was heard with significant impact in the world

185

of political life far outside the church. In its own arena the local congregation is called to this prophetic task of finding God's task, clearly describing the opposition, and pointing to the hope that is sustaining.

This word is not only addressed to the church, but sometimes must be spoken directly to the world. This was the case for the Confessing Church in Germany when, in the now famous Barmen Declaration, the church declared a ringing "no" to the pretensions of Hitler and affirmed "we repudiate the false teaching that there are areas of our life in which we belong not to Jesus Christ but to another lord." The implications of such a theological statement are made specific in an illustration by W. A. Visser 't Hooft, related by D. T. Niles:

The year 1941 gives you a good example. When the Germans were occupying Holland they asked the Church of Holland to adopt certain practices about the Jews. The Church of Holland replied, "We cannot obey you because Christ is Lord. You and we have to render our final account to him—to the final judge." Did the Nazi commandant understand what is meant? He may have or he may not have. But at least the church was talking his language. We cannot address the world unless we address it from our standpoint as those who are speaking for their lord.

We had best recognize how difficult it is for an American congregation to find much reality in these affirmations about the present reality of Christ's lordship. While I am certain that only with such a confidence is faithful missionary action long possible, it remains incredibly difficult to convey effectively the meaning and importance of this point. Hard work must be done to find ways of helping missionary congregations understand what it means to affirm that Jesus Christ is Lord of the world.

The most helpful analogy I have come upon is that of the situation during a war when the peace treaty has been signed, the victory won, but the enemy continues to fight on. Thus Japanese troops on Okinawa continued to fight long after the peace treaty had been signed in Tokyo Harbor. The American troops, well aware that a victory had been won and the war was over, were nevertheless engaged in a deadly encounter with an enemy, defeated in principle, but still vicious and dangerous. This is the position of the Christian in the world. Confident that the victory of Christ is real, he can continue to face the manifold threats of the principalities and powers of evil which still rage so furiously in the world. This kind of affirmation permits the Christian in the city to face its problems with hope. George Younger wrote, "Through the reign of Christ the power of sin is already being broken and wholeness being restored to the babel of metropolitan life. As the Redeemer who gives the city of God to men and dwells in its midst, God works out his salvation in the world as we know it." An end has been put to uncertainty about the ultimate meaning of human destiny.

The consequences of such a faith in Christ's lordship are significant for the work of a congregation in missionary tasks:

1. In the confidence that Christ is Lord and in his hands lies the future men may now live their present lives free of anxiety. An end has been put to uncertainty about the ultimate meaning of human destiny.

2. Since Christ is at work now in the world, the congregation does not set out to take him to the world as a stranger who must be introduced. Their only task is to make his power and presence known to those who do not yet have the eyes of faith.

3. When men believe that Christ is present in the world, they look for him in every area of life, both individual and corporate, expect to encounter him in their neighbor, and serve him in the normal affairs of daily life.

In order for integrity to emerge between this kind of theological affirmation and the actual witness of a congregation real time must be found in its life together to listen, to understand, and then to speak of God's power and presence to the world. Preparation continually for the prophetic role is the only way to meet crisis situations when they arise. Then the congregation may dare to stand together in its word to the world, rather than letting the minister stand often alone and unsupported. Thus in the midst of all the Protestant failure in Little Rock at the time of the crisis over schools, in one case at least the Bible study groups of a congregation did take prophetic action and in the process made it clear that it was the church speaking, not the clergy.

In the city the tensions between racial groups are obviously an important area for prophetic concern, but only one urgent need among many. What does God require of the congregation that finds itself in the midst of the heterogeneity of the city, and what is God seeking to do in the situation? Out of these questions the congregation may begin to find its proper response and understand what it must do and what it must say to itself and to the world.

The need for a prophetic voice to speak out against the pressures of modern urban life is undeniable. Here is a role the church is called to fill, weak and hesitant as its voice may be. There is little other hope of protest today except that which comes from voices of despair or bitterness. In the struggle of men for justice a voice that speaks with a transcendent perspective, with compassion and hope, is an urgent alternative to the Black Muslims or the cries of the far right. Society needs built into it the prophetic function which only the congregation alive to the workings of God in history can truly fulfill. This traditional role of the churches in American life must be recovered by missionary congregations today. Some years ago in *Christianity and Society* Charles D. Kean defined this task of the church in these words:

It is not an escape from history into a resolution of human problems on a sphere above mundane matters, nor is it a naïve confidence that some particular oversimplified solution may be superimposed on history. It is rather the illumination in depth of all concrete relationships—of family, business, neighborhood and world—so that the dimensions of responsibility and denial stand out for what they are, and in which living men and women are freed to be themselves in a real world. Thus they are able to face the twin dangers of self-deception and despair by a new confidence as reborn people who know themselves as forgiven sinners. This is good news.[8]

The Importance of Hope

As the individual in dispersion is sustained by hope, so for the congregation in its united witness its faithfulness depends upon hope in spite of the impossible tasks it faces in the midst of the modern city. No longer does the imagery of a mighty conquering army or of a world won for Christ in this generation sustain the congregation. Now the metaphor of salt or leaven is more relevant. The inner-city congregation is called to flavor, preserve, and leaven its situation, while trusting in the ultimate faithfulness of God. The gospel, in calling men to God's work, demands realism. So also, in continuing to trust in God in the midst of all discouragement and conflict, the congregation is allowed no cynicism, for it trusts in the Resurrection. Living in the midst of the world, but part of the invisible kingdom of Christ, the congregation endures, suffers, watches, confesses, perseveres, overcomes, and resists the powers of darkness. The congregation continues in its missionary task, not because in some ways it finds that conditions are gradually improving or the kingdom of God is being achieved, but simply in patient waiting for the great acts of the full revelation of the kingdom and its Lord, for a new heaven and a new earth that are the final glory of God.

Structures through which hope is affirmed and maintained are not something special, but are reflected in worship, in the small groups, and in the attitude of the congregation toward the world. Worship, essentially within the gathered life of the congregation, may also be brought out into the world as an affirmation of hope and as a way of pointing, so the world may see, to the Lord of the church. In New York City the urban parishes of the Episcopal diocese hold an annual day of witness at the Cathedral. Here is a

[8] Charles D. Kean, "Communicating the Christian Message," *Christianity and Society,* Vol. 15, No. 4 (Fall, 1950), p. 16.

dramatic meeting of Christians from all sections of the city, demonstrating their solidarity and strength. Christian festivals also provide an excellent opportunity for congregations to witness to their faith and to make clear in the midst of the world their ultimate obedience. In East Harlem the united dawn service on Easter, preceded by a march through the neighborhood, has been a significant Protestant witness in which Christians announce the joy of the Resurrection.

Through preaching and worship, Bible study and preparation for life in dispersion—in all its life—the congregation must be reminded that confidence in the Resurrection, the hope of final victory, does not cancel out the conflict of the present. Inner city congregations are learning to survive without bitterness or cynicism the knowledge that the world is not going to become a place of increasing happiness and peace. The political rule of God has stern implications. The pages of the New Testament suggest again and again that the warfare in which men are engaged, although won in principle, yet rages. Christ's victory has been won in principle, but the forces which war against him do not yet accept the fact. We must recognize that human history will be a progression to increasing strife and conflict.

That is what we are asked to expect and we can understand it. A truer vision of God will help us to a truer vision of anti-Christ. When vision was dim, conflicts between right and wrong, so called were never simply that. There was right and wrong on both sides. Both sides were gray. When gray and gray have a fight, gray always wins. As history moves on we are told to expect that white will become whiter and black will become blacker—the gray will disappear—God's light will beat down upon this world and the result will be increasing conflict between right and wrong—between God and evil—until evil is finally exposed and finally destroyed. We are now living in the kingdom of the Son in which Jesus said, "Whenever you pray, always begin your prayers, Our Father, thy kingdom come." If the Lord's Prayer begins with eschatology is something we do not like, it seems to me the only way in which we can understand history in terms of the New Testament.[9]

Issues
for Missionary Structures

The purpose of the missionary congregation is to enter into the politics of God. This purpose is fulfilled as it lives fully in the world, sustained by its gathered life of worship and preparation. In the world, as we indicated, the congregation must discover what God is doing, join in these tasks, and point to what God is doing for its own sake and for that of the world.

In concluding this chapter it is important to note that in a missionary congregation all three aspects of witness are held together—the reality of the Incarnation, the Crucifixion, and the Resurrection. Again and again, to the emasculation of its witness, the congregation takes only one of these as its basic emphasis or its mode of understanding. In the life and mission of the congregation, as in the meaning of the new humanity in Christ, all three aspects belong inseparably together. Christians believe in the Incarnation, that God is now at work in his world. Therefore, they enter in solidarity into the life of this world. They believe in the Crucifixion, that God is presently at work restoring men to their true humanity and maintaining them in this new life in his church. Therefore, they seek in every possible way to minister to their fellowmen, mediating the healing and love of Christ. They believe in the Resurrection; that is, in God's triumph over the forces of evil and dishumanity. Therefore, they live with hope and reckless joy and utter confidence.

These words must be living realities for congregations that are of God. At Amsterdam in the first meeting of the World Council of Churches the congregations of Christendom were thus addressed:

[9] D. T. Niles, "Evangelism in a World of Rapid Social Change," *The City Church* (May-June, 1960), p. 3.

Our coming together to form a World Council will be in vain unless Christians and Christian congregations everywhere commit themselves to the Lord of the Church in a new effort to seek together, where they live, to be His witnesses and servants among their neighbors. . . . We have to make of the Church in every place a voice for those who have no voice, and a home where every man will be at home. We have to learn afresh together what is the duty of the Christian man or woman in industry, in agriculture, in politics, in the professions and in the home.

Necessity of Unity

For the congregation the demands of mission make some form of grass-roots ecumenicity essential. This need has intruded itself into each of the three sections of this chapter, not as an extra asset, but as a necessary reality for faithful witness and service. It may be that in the inner city today there is enough apprehension of the urgency of this need to make some real progress possible in the face of denominational apathy or even opposition. The existence of the Inner City Protestant Parish in Cleveland, the West Side Christian Parish in Chicago, and the East Harlem Protestant Parish in New York provide some evidence of hope and some concrete illustrations of how unity may be achieved.

These parishes, however, were special creations brought into situations of Protestant vacuum. The existing congregations of an inner-city neighborhood must also learn to work in unity. In this task there is little experience anywhere, but an increasing willingness to experiment can be seen in many cities. Several clues to the development of local unity are available.

1. The clergy must discover the need for unity in mission. They cannot bring congregations to work together, but they can certainly prevent it. The present strategy of the Chicago City Missionary Society is to foment group ministries in local communities of the inner city in the hope that out of them will come mutual confidence and understanding which will make it possible for congregational unity to develop. The statement of the Ecumenical

Ministry in Englewood, Illinois, is a good example of what such a pattern might look like.[10]

2. Unity is for the sake of witness and service. Thus congregations are called to meet at the point of obedience in the world rather than at the point of confessional and doctrinal differences. Whatever may be the disagreement about baptism, for example, congregations can join in an Easter Dawn service or in working for better schools. One can surmise that only congregations whose lives are centered in mission will have the freedom and conviction to join in any kind of serious unity.

The Special Situation of the Inner City

As an inner-city congregation seeks to fulfill its missionary task, both through its laity in dispersion and corporately, it is directly confronted with the public realm much more obviously than its sister suburban churches. In suburbia the congregation's concern toward the community can easily remain completely within the privatized world of home and family. In the inner city the moment the church takes the world seriously it runs head-on into all the urgent problems of metropolitan life. Thus the peculiar relevance for the whole church of the struggle in the inner city to find missionary structures is again apparent. Obedience demands participation in public life for the sake of a human environment. Here and there inner-city congregations, by dint of vigorous lay participation in community life, through developing corporate forms of service and ministry, and through speaking the prophetic word, are learning to serve their Lord in faithfulness.

At once their own limitations in the face of the vast problems of the metropolis also become apparent. The discovery and use of missionary structures in the inner city then quickly leads to a cry for help from Protestant congregations in the whole metropolitan

[10] See Bruce D. Johnston, "The Ecumenical Ministry in Englewood," *Behold* (December, 1961).

area. Effective witness within the pyramids of power are quite out of their reach. Only as their cry is heard by the whole church do they find succor. For suburban and large downtown congregations relevant participation in the public realm will not be fulfilled by active life in their own homogeneous neighborhood, but will require an arena of involvement that encompasses the whole metropolis. In responding to the needs as defined in the inner city the whole church is called back to its task, long avoided, of seeking to witness to God's concern for the entire city and of entering into the work of making a tolerable human community. Then a servant church may reject its preoccupation with its own life and assume responsibility for obedience within the life of the world, not at all afraid of change, but willing to acknowledge God's activity in history and to confirm man's responsibility to fashion the future.

Structural Demands

For the congregation, genuine missionary involvement in the world implies a quite clear focus for its life. If it exists for mission, then the responsible governing boards must be devoted primarily to implementing the missionary work of the church and not to internal problems of maintenance. The context in which congregational decisions about corporate action in the world can be made needs to be established. Now, the congregation will have to meet not only for corporate worship, but to discover what God is requiring of his people in their situation. All this may seem very threatening in the light of present commitments to programs centered in buildings—or perhaps it merely seems unrealistic. But no talk about the missionary nature of the church will mean anything until each congregation reshapes its own structures to fulfill the mission, no matter what the discomfort or the cost. No part of a congregation's life exists for its own sake. Every part is at the disposal of God's mission.

EPILOGUE

We have been dealing with a crucial issue that is presently in the forefront of ecumenical discussion, the renewal of the church. For a good many years now prophetic voices within the church have pointed to the increasing irrelevance of the Protestant enterprise to the central issues of modern life. "A secularized church in a pseudo-Christian culture" increasingly deals only with the private and personal world of men, largely peripheral to the public realm. In Europe the problem for the church is more clear-cut and honest. Men have simply stopped bothering with the churches, a fact that is true for both Protestants and Catholics in such countries as Germany, France, England, Scotland, and in Scandinavia, where less than 10 per cent of the population has any significant congregational involvement.

In America the religious interest which has led to the extensive "churchification" of suburbia has given the impression of vast Christian vitality and of widespread commitment to a religious community. Only gradually has it become apparent to some within the church that the suburban boom may mask a serious withdrawal of Christian responsibility for the basic mission of the church. In many places in suburbia there are signs of great restlessness as men and women ask what their busyness is all about, and whether it is in fact the business of God that is demanding their energy and devotion. The books and articles that are forming a missionary theology are read widely in suburbia. Renewal in the light of these theological demands is a burning issue for conscientious pastors and laymen. Precisely at this point, restless about the superficial character of religious commitment, filled with exciting theology that has given them a new vision of the calling of God's people, they confront the problem of structures. Here is the heart of the matter, for everywhere they turn in their honest search for paths of obedience they are confronted with the rigidity of present structures of congregational life. Morphological fundamentalism emerges as the compelling problem in the renewal of the church, all the more unmanageable because of the seeming success of present church patterns in bringing vast numbers of people within the circle of the religious institution.

The peculiar relevance of the inner-city churches arises at this point. In the heart of America, face to face with the stark realities of modern urban life, they have usually tried simply to reproduce the present structures of church life in their environment—with disastrous results. The old patterns, seemingly so successful in suburbia, no longer have power to serve the church in this setting. Here the congregation cannot so easily retreat within a private realm, for the crucial issues of discrimination, education, employment, and all the rest intrude themselves forcibly. In a sense the private realm of men and women in the inner city is inseparable from the public realm. Through no virtue of their own some inner city congregations have thus been led to an honest recognition of the profound failure of traditional congregational patterns and have sought with urgency for new structures that might serve God's purpose. If, as we suggest, the inner city provides a sharp picture of the realities and the shape of modern urban life, then these inner-city parishes that are struggling in their own situation to discover the missionary structure of the congregation have a significance far beyond their own communities. In seeking for patterns of missionary validity they serve the whole church as a

196

kind of laboratory. Because their failure is so manifest these churches are often given unique freedom from traditional institutional expectations and allowed to search for new structures in many directions. In attempting to describe the present state of this search we are thus dealing with life and death issues for the whole church.

Such a statement is not meant to be pretentious. The rather meager illustrations in some of the latter chapters in this study indicate to what a large degree we have been dealing with a problem in design. It has been easier to say "the church must . . ." than to find evidence that here and there congregations are actually taking the imperatives of their theological perspective and putting them into some kind of concrete form. More important, we are as much concerned here with a method of seeking missionary structures as with specific solutions. There is no "missionary structure" but countless structures through which congregations in various times and places will fulfill their function as God's instruments in the world. Our contention is that missionary structures are neither "given" in the Bible or tradition, nor are they simply the church's response to its particular situation. Rather, missionary structures must always emerge from the dialogue, continuous and necessary, between the faith of the church and its cultural setting. On the one hand, there is the theological task. What is the purpose of the church and its ministry? What is God calling his people to be and to do? Such questions must be answered in every generation in the light of the New Testament and the history of the church. In our day, most congregations have not asked these questions at all, but simply have taken for granted that the present institutional patterns were right and appropriate. When at last these questions are asked the first discovery is often one of judgment, for most congregations have strayed far from any defensible position in light of the historic meaning of the church. Here we have been concerned to note how the emerging theological consensus does judge harshly the present life of Protestant congregations. But the more important reason for dealing with this consensus is to have a clear basis for seeking missionary structures that have theological integrity.

Equally important is the necessity for the congregation to take seriously the other half of the dialogue, with its situation in the world. The church can easily operate in a vacuum, unaware that it is out of touch with the real world of men and decisions into which it is called to enter and participate. In the inner city the congregations that have been forced to come to grips with their situation discover that they have as much to learn about the shape of the church from the world as from the Bible. They are learning again that God is at work in the city, that Christ is Lord, not just in the church, but in the world. The needs of the world, the cry of men for knowledge of their true humanity, stand as fully in judgment over the present patterns of missionary congregations as does theology. The shape of modern urban life, by the same token, must also give direction to the new forms which are necessary if God's work is to be done and the congregation once again to be engaged in mission.

The task of discovering and then living through the appropriate missionary structures for our day can begin at either point—the needs and understanding of the world or by theological reflection. We argue only that neither has a necessary priority or dominance, but that one without the other necessarily leads to serious trouble. When Christians in the city sixty years ago responded to the needs of men it was necessary to write a theology of the social gospel. Too often, however, the institutional enterprise that began with the need of man in the city lost any significant contact with theology and ended as no witness to God at all. By the same token, it is possible to evolve a brilliant and relevant theology of mission, but to find that it serves no useful purpose unless and until it is given concrete institutional expression that takes fully into account the reality of the human situation in all its particularity.

In the present historical moment, if one were to start with the needs of the world, he would stress the necessity for flexible church forms, for mobility, for a new understanding of ordination that would enable God's people to function in the world without full-time, paid, professional clergy. The questions of involvement and relevance in the world, however, quickly lead to theological discussion on the nature of the ministry, the doctrine of the laity, and a host of related issues. Or one might begin with the present structure of parochial life. Is this congregation engaged in mission? Are the laity present self-consciously in the world? Does their life in the gathered aspect of the congregation prepare them for witness and service in the world. At once, the answers demand an understanding of the context of the church in its historical and cultural setting. Thus the search for missionary structures may begin at either end but always involves the same dialogue. Sometimes renewal seems to come to a congregation that simply begins to struggle to serve in the world. The East Harlem Protestant Parish began by trying to defeat all God's enemies in East Harlem. It was driven back to Bible study, to worship, to theological study. Others begin with a new grasp of God's vision for his people and then move into missionary encounter.

But we have not said enough. We are not, ultimately, engaged in a human enterprise at all. The priority lies with God, even as we seek with all human energy and understanding to discern the shape of missionary structures for our own time. This is not simply a pious footnote. The task of this book, apart from simply reporting and describing what has been taking place, has an element of human pretentiousness. We have been concerned with a project in design, seeking to suggest what God may be calling his people to do and to be in light of the Christian traditions and the contemporary world. God will choose what forms he will use. He alone will fill a congregation with missionary conviction and the courage to serve faithfully in the world. So it must be with a certain tentativeness and humility that we describe possible missionary structures. Even today there is going on a serious debate between those who believe that some form of renewal is possible for the local congregation and others who feel that the present residentially based congregation is hopeless. Gibson Winter, for one, is convinced that morphological fundamentalism has too firm a grip ever to be loosened.[1] A World Council of Churches document asks whether the necessary missionary mobility can be recovered as long as we continue "the highly institutionalized and professionalized pattern of the ministry," a pattern not likely to be broken down in American Protestantism. Even a prophetic parish minister, Gordon Cosby, who has spent fifteen years in what is often taken to be the most vital missionary congregation in America has been led to write:

The church as we know it in our time must go. This conviction has come to me gradually—I have worked with it consciously for the past 15 years and been disturbed by it for the past three. Just a few weeks ago I crossed a line in my thinking. Now I am on the side of feeling that the institutional structures that we know are not renewable. Even where there is renewal (and this goes on in many congregations) the stance of the church is almost always the same—a stance which is contrary to the very nature of a church committed to mission.

The chorus of such voices is likely to increase in the immediate future, but their effect may well be to increase the rigidity of present patterns rather than to call churches to mission. The discontinuity with the present sounds too great, the call to obedience too radical for many to hear and heed. The conviction underlying this book is that a better point of departure is to begin with the present institutional life of the church and within that context seek to find paths of missionary obedience. Out of this struggle with the old forms may come the need for new forms, bolder and more radical than any I have suggested here. This will be a process of change that accepts continuity with the past and is able to build upon the historical faith of the church, even as it listens more emphatically to the need of the world. In other words, I argue that only as congregations seek with diligence to enter into the kind of search I have outlined in this volume and to begin to attempt such

[1] See his important volume *The New Creation as Metropolis* (New York: The Macmillan Company, 1963).

missionary structures as I have described will it be possible or seem necessary to search for forms that lie beyond our present discernment. The missionary structures outlined here are urgent next steps for the church, demanding obedience of a radical character, if they are to be taken seriously. These are perhaps only first steps— Bible study, liturgical understanding, style of life, the ministry of the laity, and the corporate witness of the congregation—the consequences of which may be the necessity for more drastic forms of Christian presence in the metropolis.

In the end we are reminded that God's gift of the Holy Spirit, empowering our structures and leading men in mission, seems to come not through the most thoughtful human solutions, but in the midst of human despair over man's efforts to solve the problems of the church. When failure comes and is accepted, then congregations may dare to rely upon God's grace alone, and in the very moment of despair may be lifted up again and given the gifts that are needed for God's mission. "If you then, who are evil, know how to give good gifts to your children, how much more will the heavenly father give the Holy Spirit to those who ask him." Thus it may be that the congregations of American Protestantism need first this gift of God-pleasing despair that makes them open again to the renewing grace of God. Insofar as the impact of the city upon Protestant congregations is to cast them into this kind of despair as they confront their failures, we may speak of the "gift of the city." The city forces upon the church the truth of the gospel, that apart from the gift of new life in Christ men do not realize their true humanity. Thus does the city lead the missionary congregation to seek old and new patterns for its life which will witness once again to the lordship of Jesus Christ over the world and in the church.

BIBLIOGRAPHY

The following bibliography, arranged in relation to the chapters of this book, indicates the main sources of understanding for the author as well as volumes that will give further insight into various issues which are raised here. In many cases a particular book will be relevant to several topics, but has been listed only under the particular chapter where it is of paramount importance. Publications of the East Harlem Protestant Parish are not listed, but a full bibliography of various articles and other materials is available from 2050 Second Avenue, New York, New York.

CHAPTER 1
THE CHALLENGE OF THE CITY

Conant, James B. *Slums and Suburbs*. New York: McGraw-Hill Book Company, 1961.

The Exploding Metropolis. The editors of *Fortune*. New York: Doubleday & Company, 1958.

Goodman, Paul. *Growing Up Absurd*. New York: Random House, 1960.

Hoover, Edgar M., and Vernon, Raymond. *Anatomy of a Metropolis*. Cambridge, Mass.: Harvard University Press, 1959.

Jacobs, Jane. *The Death and Life of Great American Cities*. New York: Random House, 1961.

Mumford, Lewis. *The City in History*. New York: Harcourt, Brace, and World, Inc., 1961.

Riesman, David. *The Lonely Crowd*. New Haven, Conn.: Yale University Press, 1950.

Whyte, William H. *The Organization Man*. New York: Simon and Schuster, Inc., 1956.

CHAPTER 2
THE CHURCH AND THE CITY

Berger, Peter L. *The Noise of Solemn Assemblies*. New York: Doubleday & Company, 1961.

The City, God's Gift to the Church. New York: Division of Evangelism, Board of National Missions, United Presbyterian Church, USA, 1961.

Herberg, Will. *Protestant-Catholic-Jew*. New York: Doubleday & Company, 1955.

Kloetzli, Walter, editor. *Challenge and Response in the City*. Rock Island, Ill.: Augustana Press, 1962.

Lee, Robert, editor. *Cities and Churches*. Philadelphia: The Westminster Press, 1962.

Marty, Martin. *The New Shape of American Religion*. New York: Harper & Row, Publishers, 1959.

Moore, Paul. *The Church Reclaims the City*. Greenwich, Conn.: The Seabury Press, 1963.

Musselman, G. Paul. *The Church on the Urban Frontier*. Greenwich, Conn.: The Seabury Press, Inc., 1960.

Webber, George W. *God's Colony in Man's World*. Nashville: Abingdon Press, 1960.

Wickham, E. R. *Church and People in an Industrial City*. London: Lutterworth Press, 1957.

Winter, Gibson. *The Suburban Captivity of the Churches*. Garden City: Doubleday & Company, 1961.

CHAPTER 3
THE EMERGING THEOLOGICAL CONSENSUS

Barth, Markus. *The Broken Wall*. Valley Forge, Pa.: Judson Press, 1959.

Lehmann, Paul. *Ethics in a Christian Context*. New York: Harper & Row, Publishers, 1963.

Niebuhr, H. Richard. *Christ and Culture*. New York: Harper & Brothers, 1951.

Reflections on a Theology of Evangelism. World Council of Churches Bulletin. Vol. V, No. 1-2, Nov., 1959.

Stringfellow, William. *A Private and Public Faith*. Grand Rapids: William B. Eerdmans Publishing Company, 1962.

Williams, Colin. *Where in the World*. New York: National Council of Churches, 1963.

Wilmore, Gayraud S. *The Secular Relevance of the Church*. Philadelphia: The Westminster Press, 1962.

Younger, George. *The Bible Calls for Action*. Valley Forge, Pa.: Judson Press, 1959.

CHAPTER 4
THE LIVING COVENANT

Barth, Karl. *The Word of God and the Word of Man*. Translated by Douglas Horton. Boston: Pilgrim Press, 1928.

De Dietrich, Suzanne. *God's Unfolding Purpose*. Philadelphia: The Westminster Press, 1960.

Dodd, C. H. *The Apostolic Preaching and Its Development*. New York: Harper & Row, Publishers, 1936.

Kraemer, Hendrik. *Communication of the Christian Faith*. Philadelphia: The Westminster Press, 1956.

Minear, Paul S. *Eyes of Faith*. Philadelphia: The Westminster Press, 1946.

CHAPTER 5
WORSHIP IN A MISSIONARY CONGREGATION

Abba, Raymond. *Principles of Christian Worship*. New York: Oxford University Press, 1957.

Davies, J. G., *et al*. *An Experimental Liturgy*. Richmond: John Knox Press, 1958.

Forsyth, P. T. *The Church and the Sacraments*. London: Independent Press, 1917.

Hebert, A. G. *Liturgy and Society*. London: Faber & Faber, Ltd., 1935.

Michonneau, G., Abbé. *Revolution in a City Parish*. Westminster, Md.: The Newman Press, 1950.

Shands, Alfred R. *The Liturgical Movement and the Local Church*. London: Student Christian Movement Press, 1959.

CHAPTER 6
THE STYLE OF LIFE IN THE CONGREGATION

Ayres, Francis O. *The Ministry of the Laity*. Philadelphia: The Westminster Press, 1962.

Bonhoeffer, Dietrich. *Life Together*. Translated by John W. Doberstein. New York: Harper & Row, Publishers, 1954.

Casteel, John, editor. *Spiritual Renewal through Personal Groups*. New York: Association Press, 1957.

Ellul, Jacques. *The Presence of the Kingdom*. Translated by Olive Wyon. Philadelphia: The Westminster Press, 1951.

Emerick, Samuel, editor. *Spiritual Renewal for Methodism*. Nashville: Methodist Evangelistic Materials, 1958.

Jenkins, Daniel. *The Protestant Ministry Today*. London: Faber & Faber, Ltd., 1958.

Johnson, Robert Clyde, editor. *The Church and Its Changing Ministry*. Philadelphia: Office of the General Assembly, United Presbyterian Church, USA, 1961.

Thurian, Max. *Confession*. London: Student Christian Movement Press, 1958.

CHAPTER 7
THE MINISTRY OF THE LAITY

Come, Arnold B. *Agents of Reconciliation*. Philadelphia: The Westminster Press, 1960.

Congar, Yves. *Lay People in the Church*. Translated by Donald Attwater. Westminster, Md.: Newman Press, 1957.

Kraemer, Hendrik. *A Theology of the Laity*. Philadelphia: The Westminster Press, 1959.

Manson, T. W. *Ministry and Priesthood: Christ's and Ours*. Richmond: John Knox Press, 1958.

Weber, Hans-Ruedi. *Salty Christians*. Greenwich, Conn.: The Seabury Press, 1963.

CHAPTER 8
THE CONGREGATION IN MISSION

Blauw, Johannes. *The Missionary Nature of the Church*. New York: McGraw-Hill Book Company, 1962.

MacLeod, George F. *Only One Way Left*. Glasgow: Iona Community Publishing House, 1956.

Maury, Philippe. *Politics and Evangelism*. Translated by Marguerite Wieser. New York: Doubleday & Company, 1959.

Newbigin, Lesslie. *The Household of God*. New York: Friendship Press, 1954.

Niles, D. T. *Upon the Earth*. New York: McGraw-Hill Book Company, 1962.

Robinson, J. A. T. *On Being the Church in the World*. London: Student Christian Movement Press, 1960.

Spike, Robert. *In But Not of the World*. New York: Association Press, 1957.

Younger, George. *The Church and the Urban Power Structures*. Philadelphia: The Westminster Press, 1963.

EPILOGUE

Allen, Roland. *Missionary Methods: St. Paul's or Ours*. London: World Dominion Press, 1960. (Original edition, 1912.)

——————. *The Spontaneous Expansion of the Church*. London: World Dominion Press, 1960. (Original edition, 1927.)

Bonhoeffer, Dietrich. *The Cost of Discipleship*. Translated by R. H. Fuller. London: Student Christian Movement Press, 1959.

——————. *Prisoner for God*. Translated by Reginald H. Fuller. New York: The Macmillan Company, 1954.

A Tent-Making Ministry. Geneva: Division of World Mission and Evangelism, World Council of Churches, 1962.

Visser 't Hooft, W. A. *The Renewal of the Church*. Philadelphia: The Westminster Press, 1957.

West, Charles C. *Outside the Camp*. New York: Doubleday & Company, 1959.

Winter, Gibson. *The New Creation as Metropolis*. New York: Doubleday & Company, 1963.

SIGNS OF RENEWAL:
CONGREGATIONS IN MISSION

Allan, Tom. *The Face of My Parish*. New York: Harper & Row, Publishers, 1957. (Glasgow, Scotland.)

Fackre, Gabriel, and Dorothy. *Under the Steeple*. Nashville: Abingdon Press, 1957. (Milltown, near Pittsburgh.)

MacLeod, George F. *We Shall Rebuild*. Glasgow: The Iona Community, rev. ed., 1962. (Iona Community.)

Morton, T. R. *The Iona Community Story*. Glasgow: The Iona Community Publishing House, 1957. (Iona Community.)

Myers, C. Kilmer. *Light the Dark Streets*. Greenwich, Conn. The Seabury Press, 1957. (Lower East Side, New York City.)

O'Connor, Elizabeth. *Call to Commitment*. New York: Harper & Row, Publishers, 1963. (Church of the Saviour, Washington, D.C.)

Raines, Robert. *New Life in the Church*. New York: Harper & Row, Publishers, 1961. (Aldersgate Methodist, Ohio.)

Southcott, Ernest. *The Parish Comes Alive*. New York: Morehouse-Barlow Company, 1956. (Leeds, England.)

IMPORTANT AND RELEVANT PERIODICALS

Christianity and Crisis. 537 W. 121st Street, New York, New York.

The Church in Metropolis. National Council of Churches, 475 Riverside Drive, New York, New York.

Concept. World Council of Churches, 475 Riverside Drive, New York, New York.

The Coracle. Iona Community, 214 Clyde Street, Glasgow, Scotland.

The Laity. World Council of Churches, 19 Route de Malagnou, Geneva, Switzerland.

Newsletter. East Harlem Protestant Parish, 2050 Second Avenue, New York, New York.

Renewal. The Community Renewal Society, 116 S. Michigan, Chicago, Illinois.